From Harare to Porto Alegre

i

ii

**An Illustrated Account of the Life
of the World Council of Churches**

December 1998 to February 2006

From Harare to Porto Alegre
1998-2006

World Council of Churches, Geneva

Photo credits

Pages 1 (bottom), 2, 4, 6, 9 (left), 13, 18, 21, 23 (both), 24, 26, 28, 29, 30, 31 (top), 32, 33, 34, 35, 36, 38, 39, 40, 41, 43, 44, 45, 47 (both), 48 (both), 49, 50 (top), 51, 52, 53, 55 (right), 56, 57, 58, 59 (left), 60 (bottom right), 61, 62, 63 (right), 67, 68, 72, 73, 74, 76, 78, 84, 87 (top and bottom), 89, 90, 91 (left), 92 (both), 93, 94, 95, 96, 97, 101, 103, 104, 108, 109, 116 (both), 117, 120, 121, 130, 131 (both), 137, 138, 141 (top), 145, 148, 150, 151, 152, 154, 158, 160, 161, 164, 166, 189: *Peter Williams/WCC*

Pages 1 (top), 54, 83 (both), 119 (right), 136 (left), 162-63: *Eduardo Quadros/WCC*

Pages 7, 15, 37, 59 (right), 60 (top), 63 (left), 64, 65, 66 (top), 85, 88, 91 (left), 98, 99, 100, 102 (both), 106 (left), 111, 114, 115 (bottom), 118 (both), 119 (left), 129, 132, 133, 140, 147, 149 (both), 163 (right): *Paul Jeffrey/ACT International*

Pages 8, 9 (right), 10: *Andreas Schölzer/WCC*

Pages 11, 31 (bottom), 70, 71, 81, 113, 122 (top), 124, 144: *Chris Black/WCC*

Page 19: *Marta Luksza*

Page 20: *Henna Aaltonen/WCC*

Page 22: *L'Osservatore Romano*

Pages 25, 55 (left): *Juan Michel/WCC*

Pages 27, 112: *Paulino Menezes/WCC & LWF*

Page 42: *Dmytro Shevchuk*

Pages 66 (bottom), 110: *Marc French/WCC*

Page 75: *Jeremy Routledge/EAPPI*

Pages 79, 87 (middle), 159, 162 (left), 173: *Catherine Alt/WCC*

Page 80: unattributed

Page 82: *Hans Ucko*

Page 86: *Joel/EAPPI*

Page 105: *Orla Clinton/Church of Sweden/ACT International*

Page 106: (right) *Mike DuBose/UMNS/ACT International*

Page 107: *Daniel Fekete/HIA/ACT International*

Pages 122 (bottom), 123: *Paul Weinberg/WCC*

Page 127: *Eva Halling/EAPPI*

Page 128: *Didier Rüf/WCC*

Page 134: *Ida Suhrke/EAPPI*

Page 135: EAPPI

Page 136: (right) *Hege Opseth/NCA/ACT International*

Page 139: *Adrián Stehlik/WCC*

Page 141 (bottom): *Christoph Gocke/EAPPI*

Page 142: *Jonathan Frerichs/ACT International*

Page 143: *Matt Robson/EAPPI*

Page 146: unattributed

The WCC central committee expresses its gratitude to Sara Speicher for her creative efforts in coordinating the preparation this report, working closely with each team to interpret the Council's vision and actions in our continuing quest for Christian unity and proclamation of God's reign.

Original: English. This publication is also available in French, German and Spanish.

Cover and design: Marie Arnaud Snakkers
Cover photos: Paul Jeffrey/ACT International, Peter Williams/WCC, Paul Weinberg/WCC, Chris Black/WCC, Juan Michel/WCC, Hege Opseth NCA/ACT International

ISBN 2-8254-1456-5

Contents

executive committee to look at the concerns expressed about membership and representation. In receiving the reports of the Special Commission and the membership study committee, the central committee approved a new category of membership, that of "churches in association with the WCC", while removing the category of "associate member churches" which had been primarily for churches which could not meet minimum size criteria.

The Special Commission recognized that the churches-in-association category may allow some churches to "step back" from membership in the Council. But there are also many churches, at present not members of the Council, which may see the status of "churches in association" as a place to draw closer to the Council in order to explore the possibilities of full membership. The hope is that the fellowship may be broadened in significant ways.

Theological criteria to be considered for membership were also added. Among these criteria, member churches are invited to "acknowledge the need to move towards the recognition of the baptism of other churches". This is another step forward regarding the emphasis placed on baptism during the period under review (see also study documents of the Joint Working Group between the Roman Catholic Church and the WCC, and of Faith and Order).

Furthermore, groups of churches in a confession or region are encouraged to apply for membership together to witness to their common calling – or to resolve the criteria of size. Applications for membership would be considered solely at central committee meetings rather than also at the assembly.

The resulting necessary revisions to the WCC constitution and rules were approved at the 2003 central committee and will have final confirmation at the ninth assembly.

Visiting the churches

Governing body members and staff of the WCC have undertaken visits to churches and other religious bodies in different parts of the world, just as thousands of Christians from various constituencies have been welcomed to the Ecumenical Centre in Geneva. This exchange of visits serves to improve understanding and deepen relationships within the ecumenical movement. The international "living letters" delegation which visited the churches in the USA in the aftermath of September 11 is a significant

Procession following celebration of the holy liturgy in the Armenian Apostolic church of the Saviour of the Nations in Shoushi, Nagorno-Karabagh.

21

example of strengthening the fellowship through the cooperative efforts of several WCC teams and partners outside and inside the USA. Other visits, such as to the China Christian Council in 2003 following its election of new leadership, help build new ecumenical relationships and open important sharing on issues such as mission and ecumenical education.

Most visible are the official visits of the WCC general secretary to member churches, often offering pastoral solidarity and assessing possibilities for international ecumenical support in situations of long-term conflict and struggle.

During his 11 years as general secretary, Konrad Raiser paid official visits to churches in 77 different countries in all the regions. In the first year of his service as general secretary, Samuel Kobia made official visits to churches in 15 different countries.

The WCC also sends official representatives to the assemblies of the regional ecumenical organizations and, when possible, the Christian world communions.

Relations with the Roman Catholic Church

Since 1965 a Joint Working Group (JWG) between the Roman Catholic Church and the WCC has met regularly. The JWG is a forum to review and initiate collaborative efforts between various programmes of the WCC and the holy see, as well as to engage in studies of common concerns which block "full koinonia" between the Roman Catholic Church and WCC member churches.

The eighth report of the JWG includes three study documents: "Ecclesiological and Ecumenical Implications of a Common Baptism", "The Nature and Purpose of Ecumenical Dialogue" and "Roman

General secretary Samuel Kobia, having represented the Council at the funeral of Pope John Paul II in April 2005, led a WCC delegation to meet with newly installed Pope Benedict XVI at the Vatican in June.

Catholic Participation in National and Regional Councils of Churches". These studies, along with the report, will be forwarded to the Pontifical Council for Promoting Christian Unity and the WCC's ninth assembly.

The studies are to be read in the wider context of the ecumenical movement today. The JWG, which had begun its work in 1965 by reflecting on the nature of dialogue, explored again the nature and practice of ecumenical dialogue in light of the experiences of thirty years, and of new challenges and opportunities for dialogue at the beginning of the third millennium.

The purpose of the study on baptism is to assist churches to recognize what has been accomplished, and to build on it. The document reviews important aspects of the growing convergence on baptism, noting the differences that remain, and illus-

trates the ecumenical impact of what has been achieved by showing examples of the way common perspectives on baptism have helped foster changed relationships, in some cases full communion, between churches long separated.

The study on Roman Catholic participation in national and regional councils of churches recognizes that in many regions of the world councils of churches are a primary means whereby relationships among churches are nurtured and advanced. The document offers rich inspiration to the reflection process on the reconfiguration of the ecumenical movement.

This period has been particularly marked by significant moments, such as leadership meetings and bilateral visits. The leadership of the Pontifical Council for Promoting Christian Unity and of the WCC met twice in

Below left: Morning worship at the central committee meeting in Potsdam, February 2001. Cardinal Georg Sterzinsky of Berlin and Dr Frieda Mangunson of Indonesia.

Below right: Hundreds of people from nearby villages came to Yirol to welcome WCC general secretary Konrad Raiser, who visited Sudan in July 2002.

23

Antelias, Lebanon, in 2000 and 2004, to welcome new persons in key positions, to assess the state of the relationship and to discuss matters of common concern.

Several contacts were renewed or established with various offices of the Roman curia, especially through visits to Geneva and to Rome. The celebration of the year 2000 offered possibilities to participate in events organized by the Roman Catholic Church.

Common reflection on the reconfiguration of the ecumenical movement and commitment in exploring the potential of the global Christian forum continue.

An event marking the fortieth anniversary of the JWG is planned for November 2005. In addition to celebrating four decades of cooperation, the event will assess progress in the ecumenical movement, the implications of the JWG on the larger reconfiguration of the ecumenical movement, and the relevance of its mandate given the changing context of the world.

Dialogue with Pentecostal, Evangelical and Independent churches

While the WCC has some Pentecostal churches among its members, the vast majority of this quickly growing segment of the global Christian faith remains outside – and often critical – of the WCC fellowship. The Harare assembly approved the formation of a WCC-Pentecostal Joint Consultative Group, which continues a dialogue that began in the mid-1990s.

Around twenty theologians and church representatives formed the Joint Consultative Group which met five times between assemblies. From the first meeting, which examined

Seeking the guidance of the Holy Spirit and in response to the invitation of the eighth assembly of the World Council of Churches, we have come together. We believe the purposes of our group are:

• to search for better ways of understanding one another;

• to look for new opportunities for mutual learning and action;

• to share our experience of Christian witness with one another;

• to discuss our challenges with the hope of moving beyond them;

• to share what we will learn with our respective churches;

leading to our affirmation of the common life in the Spirit.

"Sing and make music in your heart to the Lord, always giving thanks to God the Father for everything in the name of the Lord Jesus Christ" (Eph. 5:19-20).

From the report of the first meeting of the Joint Consultative Group between the WCC and Pentecostals in June 2000

24

the way Pentecostals and WCC member churches perceive each other, discussions moved on to theological issues related to unity – areas of convergence and divergence among them or their respective churches.

Pentecostals raised concerns about the World Council of Churches, such as its apparent over-emphasis on a social agenda at the expense of evangelism. At the same time, WCC members sought to understand the theme of unity in light of the dramatic growth of Pentecostals, sometimes at the expense of the more traditional churches.

The group took advantage of meeting in different locations with different hosts – France, Ecuador, South Korea, USA and South Africa – to experience different church traditions and communities to give context to their discussions.

A report from the Joint Consultative Group will be presented to the ninth assembly, which will determine if such a dialogue will continue.

The eighth assembly also encouraged the WCC and its member churches to continue to search for new ways to relate to Evangelicals and draw on the many Evangelicals within and outside the WCC and its member churches. In addition to discussion around the global Christian forum, a series of consultations have encouraged discussion with some of these churches and related organizations.

The WCC also cooperates with the Organization of African Instituted Churches, and has strengthened links with the Council of Christian Communities of an African Approach in Europe. Most of the African Christian communities in Europe are charismatic or Pentecostal and many are related to African Instituted Churches.

Left: Members of the African Church of the Holy Spirit gather by the roadside in Karan, Kenya, before marching to their place of worship in Bul Bul, April 2004.

Right: An ecumenical celebration of commitment and planning for the ninth assembly, during a preparatory session in Porto Alegre, Brazil, 9 November 2004.

Regional ecumenical organizations have been formed in all parts of the world except North America where the national councils of churches in the USA and in Canada are generally considered as regional ecumenical organizations. They may send representatives to WCC assemblies and to meetings of the central committee.

- All Africa Conference of Churches
- Christian Conference of Asia
- Caribbean Conference of Churches
- Conference of European Churches
- Latin American Council of Churches
- Middle East Council of Churches
- Pacific Conference of Churches

Progress towards a global Christian forum

At the Harare assembly, practical steps to widen the fellowship focused on the proposal of a "forum" that would bring together Roman Catholics, Pentecostals and Evangelicals for occasional joint meetings with WCC member churches to enable all participants to move together with a sense of Christian unity.

The assembly encouraged the central committee to continue discussion with leaders of various bodies that are interested in such a forum – noting that care must be taken clearly to distinguish the nature and purpose of this forum versus the WCC, and the distinctive ecclesiastical and organizational nature of other bodies.

Careful discussions brought together representatives of churches that have not previously gathered together, including Orthodox, Catholic, Protestant, Anglican, Evangelical and Pentecostal traditions.

A series of regional consultations were held beginning in 2004 to explore with the leaders of a diverse cross-section of churches and ecumenical organizations the possibilities of engaging them in common reflection and action on their witness and unity.

The goal is to host a truly representative global Christian gathering – a global Christian forum – in 2007.

With efforts still so new, it is not surprising that major hurdles remain. While many regional and global leaders are enthusiastic, raising awareness and gaining support from their respective governing bodies is itself a long process. And with the

A choir leads morning devotions at the Athens conference on world mission and evangelism (CWME), May 2005.

goal of having a forum representative of all Christian traditions, efforts must continue to expand participation, particularly from the Evangelical community.

Yet the progress, optimism and consensus achieved so far in consultations and within various organizations are remarkable, and bode well for this new expression of Christian unity initiated by the WCC.

Fostering the coherence of the ecumenical movement

The Harare assembly had asked for reflection on a common ecumenical agenda and the integration of global and regional structures.

Consultations with regional and national ecumenical organizations have been one way to consider the role and functions of the varying ecumenical bodies and work towards minimizing duplication of materials and programmes.

The general secretaries of the WCC and the regional ecumenical organizations (REOs) meet annually to discuss such collaboration, including the reconfiguration of the ecumenical movement. The WCC and the REO general secretaries also initiated a joint meeting with ecumenical partner agencies and specialized ministries to build a better understanding about multilateral and bilateral relationships, functions and support. The establishment of liaison groups between the WCC and some of the REOs (the Conference of European Churches, the Christian Conference of Asia, the Latin American Council of Churches) has proved to be an effective means to consolidate close relationships.

Several consultations with general secretaries of national councils of churches in association with the WCC were held to support the common commitment to ecumenism, explore models of conciliar ecumenism, and assess trends and needs. Of the more than 110 national councils which exist worldwide, over sixty are associated with the WCC, 33 are affiliated with the Conference on World Mission and Evangelism and most of the others maintain a working relationship with the Council. The assembly had encouraged such discussions in order to learn from each other and work together in "the implementation and ownership of the ecumenical commitment locally and nationally, within the framework of the CUV".

The Harare assembly also recommended a process to strengthen relationships between the WCC and

The ecumenical coalition at the World Social Forum marches through the streets of Porto Alegre, January 2005.

27

It is impossible to speak of the World Council of Churches apart from the ecumenical movement out of which it grew and of which it is a highly visible part. While the ecumenical movement is wider than its organizational expressions, and while the WCC is essentially the fellowship of its member churches, it serves at the same time as a prominent instrument and expression of the ecumenical movement. As such, it is an advocate of the impulse for renewal which has characterized the movement from its beginnings.

Towards a Common Understanding and Vision

"If there is no structure of reference, no transparency in the way responsibilities are exercised, nor any discipline about participation, we risk encouraging the rise of a militant, populist and fundamentalist Christianity. The World Council of Churches can be, in its own way, such a fundamental framework or backbone. Its future also lies in the way it allows for the expression of the widest possible diversity of opinion, in the way it provides a protected space for encounter, in the resistance it offers to normative, exclusive and trenchant ways of thinking. The challenge for tomorrow's WCC lies precisely in accompanying changes in mentalities, in generations and in forms of Christianity and in facing up to the spiritual challenges that result."

Rev. Dr Konrad Raiser,
November 2003

Christian world communions (CWCs). The WCC participates regularly in the work of the Christian world communions' conference of secretaries as well as in the Geneva-based WCC-Lutheran World Federation-World Alliance of Reformed Churches staff group.

In 2004, the staff group communicated to their respective general secretaries the results of the evaluation of three joint programmatic activities: violence against women, economic globalization, and HIV/AIDS. The responses to the evaluation pointed to a strong affirmation of the value of close programmatic cooperation in the areas concerned. They also provided valuable perspectives on the different and complementary roles of the cooperating partners, especially between the WCC on the one hand and the CWCs on the other. However, the responses also revealed that a more complete description of these different and complementary roles would be useful, both for the continued programmatic cooperation and for the configuration of the ecumenical movement.

Indeed, clarifying roles of varied ecumenical actors, working towards holding common assemblies and striving for a common ecumenical agenda have become central topics in the "reconfiguration" discussion.

Discussing the reconfiguration of the ecumenical movement

The consultations with ecumenical partner bodies, and challenges arising from a changing global situation, have highlighted the increasing pressures on churches and ecumenical organizations. At the initiative of WCC general secretary Konrad Raiser, and after consideration by the central committee in 2003, the WCC convened a meeting in Antelias, Lebanon, in November 2003 to discuss a "new configuration" of the ecumenical movement that would strengthen relationships among all the various actors in the ecumenical movement.

Following the announcement of the vote, WCC general secretary-elect Samuel Kobia is congratulated by WCC general secretary Konrad Raiser. Central committee meeting, Geneva, 27 August 2003. Dr Kobia took office in January 2004.

The meeting of church leaders, ecumenists, theologians, youth and social scientists – invited in their individual capacities – offered reflections on the challenges and vision of the ecumenical movement, and understandings of what "reconfiguration" means. The consultation called for a broad, participatory discussion, facilitated by the WCC, with churches, ecumenical partners and potential partners.
More than one hundred partici-

pants from WCC member churches, national and regional councils of churches, Christian world communions, the Roman Catholic Church and Pentecostal churches as well as from church-related agencies came together to share their visions of ecumenism and to seek more effective ways for the churches to work together in today's changing global context.

The consultation's final statement emphasized the urgency of seeking new forms of ecumenism. It also underlined the WCC's role to provide a forum for "exchange and common advocacy against injustice", to "foster accountability in the quality of relationships among churches and partners", and to "provide space for the ecumenical movement to formulate a common ecumenical vision for the 21st century".

Practical recommendations were also made to clarify the respective roles of existing ecumenical organizations at international, regional and national levels, as well as the roles and relationships of specialized ministries and agencies within the ecumenical movement. A consultative process was recommended to strengthen relationships with Christian world communions and explore "the nature and form of a common assembly or process" that would further the goal of a common ecumenical agenda.

Strengthening the ways in which existing ecumenical actors work together can and should be done in such a way as to invite others into the process, rather than create further barriers between Christian organizations. Similarly, ecumenical developments between churches not only deepen relationships between them but also contribute to greater coherence in the common work. By focusing on the way in which ecumenical actors relate to one another, we hope to become more effective in our ministries and to be better witnesses to the God we seek to serve.

"Reflections from Antelias": Consultation on Reconfiguration of the Ecumenical Movement, November 2003

Supporting participation and leadership of youth

The programme guidelines committee at the Harare assembly emphasized that work with young people needs to be "significantly strengthened" through ecumenical formation, internships, stewards programme, pre-meeting orientations – accompanied by greater participation of young people in decision-making bodies. The concern has been reiterated on a number of occasions by the central committee that the WCC take more seriously the important role and valuable contribution of youth in its life and work.

Youth participants in the Athens CWME perform their interpretation of the conference theme, "Come, Holy Spirit, Heal and Reconcile", May 2005.

The survival of the ecumenical movement is intrinsically related to the involvement of a younger generation who are capable of bringing new perspectives and enthusiasm that will deepen and broaden the fellowship of churches within the WCC. It is not only about involving youth in ecumenical work through the youth desk, nor about programmes directed specifically at youth, nor about quotas. The need across all programmes is to develop theological principles to ensure the full participation of young people. Ecumenical leadership training is essential for the life of the ecumenical movement.

30 **Programme report** *from central committee, 2001*

A youth group gathers at the St Mina Coptic Orthodox monastery in Luanda, Kenya, in April 2004.

Youth are vital in re-energizing the ecumenical movement and leading the movement into the future. With youth officially defined as those aged 18-30, many youth are already leaders in churches and ecumenical organizations. Thus the WCC works both to include youth in ongoing programmes as well as provide opportunities for ecumenical formation and leadership training.

Through youth consultations and involvement, youth have been integrated into many programmes and activities such as economic globalization, climate change, missiological and theological study and reflection, interfaith peace and conflict resolution, and the reconfiguration of the ecumenical movement.

The WCC and the World Student Christian Federation held a joint ecumenical leadership training and formation seminar for 32 young people in 2001 in Cuba. The seminar was

designed to motivate participants to organize local ecumenical projects together within their own communities. An award-winning WCC video and DVD, *Facing the Future*, shows the learning and the challenges that grow out of such ecumenical encounters. The WCC and its ecumenical partners follow and support individuals from those encounters who seek to be more fully involved in ecumenical work at national, regional and international levels.

The World Youth Programme (WYP) equips young people to respond to the challenges of their situation in church and society. The WYP supports projects in sectors such as ecumenical leadership development, overcoming violence and HIV/AIDS. More than fifty programmes involving thousands of youth are initiated through the WYP each year.

The WCC internship programme hosts small groups of young people for a

year at the Ecumenical Centre in Geneva to work on particular programmes. Over twenty young people have served as WCC interns in the period 1999 through 2005. The young people bring fresh insights to the work of the WCC, while learning more about ecumenism and the role of the WCC in the ecumenical movement.

The WCC's stewards programme is a unique leadership training opportunity for young people from different churches and different parts of the world. It seeks to educate young people about ecumenism so that they can initiate ecumenical youth programmes when they return to their home country. The programme brought more than two hundred young people from all over the world not only to assist with major meetings such as central committees and the world mission conference but also, in a new initiative since Harare, to participate in a one-week ecumenical leadership training seminar.

An ecumenical youth website was developed and a "young leaders on-line" project in cooperation with the Vesper Society in the USA developed tools and methods for a global ecumenical youth community on the internet.

While the leadership and participation of youth in programmes across the WCC can be celebrated, it is clear that much more needs to be done to make their inclusion the norm rather than a special effort. Even more, ensuring at least minimum levels of youth representation on governing bodies and in major meetings requires ongoing commitment by church leadership. With such commitment, the voice and vision of the future of the ecumenical movement can be present today.

Youth programme based in the Justice, Peace and Creation team

We dream of an ecumenical movement where young people, with all their talents and skills, take an active part and leadership in all its dimensions…The ecumenical movement started with young people taking leadership in the last century (WSCF, YMCA, YWCA). This reminds us of the important role young people can play.

Visions from Youth Consultation on *Reconfiguration of the Ecumenical Movement, November 2003*

31

Stewards from many countries and regions of the world undertake ecumenical journeys to provide essential assistance and energy at such meetings as the Harare assembly of 1998 (left) and the 2005 Geneva meeting of the WCC central committee (above).

Special Commission on Orthodox Participation in the WCC

In the period leading up to the Harare assembly, two Orthodox churches, Bulgaria and Georgia, withdrew from WCC membership. In May 1998, Eastern Orthodox churches gathered in Thessaloniki, Greece, enumerated a number of serious concerns and demanded the establishment of a "mixed commission" with the WCC to consider the grievances and propose lasting solutions.

The Harare assembly established a Special Commission on Orthodox Participation in the WCC with the mandate "to study and analyze the whole spectrum of issues related to Orthodox participation in the WCC" and "to make proposals concerning the necessary changes in structure, style and ethos of the Council".

Half of the sixty members of the Commission came from the Eastern and Oriental Orthodox churches, and the others from the rest of the WCC's member churches. As the Commission began its work, it quickly became clear that many of the issues named by the Orthodox were shared by a broad spectrum of churches in a reflection already begun through the Common Understanding and Vision process. (A commentary on the CUV document is Appendix A to this report.)

The Special Commission, in the end, dealt in very concrete terms with the implications of the Common Understanding and Vision process. The process of the Special Commission has thus allowed WCC member churches an opportunity to pursue and strengthen their reflection on the very nature of the WCC and the fellowship of churches.

The Special Commission began its work in December 1999. Over the next three years, the Commission met in four full plenary sessions, and divided its work into four sub-committees, which studied some of the issues in depth. As one of the goals of the Special Commission was to foster an increased mutual understanding of the churches and their life, the locations of meetings were chosen bearing in mind the potential for church visits and encounters.

The final report of the Special Commission was received by the central committee in 2002. Discussions at the committee meeting and afterwards were intense, as the issues addressed are at the heart of ecumenism as a movement encompassing many traditions.

The recommendations adopted by the central committee addressed ecclesiology, social and ethical issues, worship and common prayer, business procedures and membership.

32

"The Special Commission has put into place an agenda which is comprehensive enough to deal even with our own understandings of the nature of the church. I should add that this change would not have been possible without the recognition that the predominant Protestant tradition still has too much influence over what gets onto our agenda, our way of working, the way we make decisions or celebrate worship. Perhaps we needed this crisis in order to understand that the Orthodox do not feel at home in the ecumenical movement as we do. Thus this painful crisis will have been beneficial by allowing a deepening of the understanding of the WCC as a 'fellowship of churches'."

Rev. Dr Konrad Raiser,
November 2003

Ecclesiology

The Special Commission report seeks to clarify two basic understandings of how WCC member churches relate to the one church of Christ. Some identify their own church with the one church. Others see their own church as a part of the one church. The Faith and Order Commission was given the task of studying more fully the implications of these self-understandings within its ongoing work in the area of ecclesiology.

Social and ethical issues

The Special Commission recognized that aspects of the WCC's public witness have been of great value for all the churches and for many outside the churches. Yet it questioned how a diverse fellowship of churches can truly find a common witness to the world.

The final report underlines that before the churches can speak out together, they need to form a common mind, wherever possible, and the WCC is a unique instrument to enable this coming together. The Special Commission believes that consensus decision-making "will make it easier for all to participate fully in the discussion of any burning ethical and social issue" and therefore may enable the forming of a common mind and a common voice.

Common prayer

The Christians gathered together in the WCC have always sought to pray together, and this time has often been the most meaningful and moving to many as a sign of our unity. For others, it has been in worship where division among Christians is most apparent.

The Orthodox voiced increasing concerns about the nature of ecumenical worship and the implication of the fact that the WCC is a gathering of churches, not a church in itself.

In a brutally divided world, churches have developed different ecclesial cultures, but by accepting the disciplines of the fellowship of the World Council of Churches they are called to acknowledge the necessity to witness together to their Christian faith, to unity in Christ and to a community with no other limits than the whole human race.

Final report of the Special Commission

p.32: A distinctive Coptic Orthodox cross in the hand of Fr Pishoy Musungu of the St Abanoub Coptic Orthodox church near Kisumu, Kenya.

Below: Sister Mathilda in the chapel of the St Mina Coptic Orthodox monastery in Kenya.

34

The holy liturgy is celebrated in the St Nikolas Chernoostrosky Orthodox women's monastery, Maloyaroslavets, Russia.

The Special Commission affirmed the primary importance of the call to pray together and the necessity of prayer as a foundation for the fellowship of churches. A framework for common prayer at ecumenical gatherings was proposed, intended primarily for the most publicized meetings of the WCC, such as assemblies, central committees and the world mission conference.

The framework identifies areas of sensitivity and proposes ways of working towards a common spiritual life in which all churches can participate in good conscience. The framework attempts to strengthen ecclesiological clarity, avoiding ambiguities which pose problems for some churches.

The Special Commission thus distinguishes between "worship" which is primarily related to a church tradition, and "common prayer" when Christians come together to pray. In some languages, "worship" implies a liturgical service or eucharist, while intercommunion is not acceptable for the Orthodox churches.

The report then differentiates between "confessional prayer", where one church offers its own tradition or practice to the whole gathering, and "interconfessional prayer", where the gifts of different traditions are combined.

In receiving the recommendation, the central committee emphasized that it is "a framework, not a prescription or even guidelines".

Praying together

Järvenpää, Finland, June 2002

It is the last session of the last plenary meeting of the Special Commission on Orthodox Participation in the WCC. The three-year journey of the Commission is coming to its end. The sixty members of the Commission have already finalized – and they, themselves, have adopted by consensus – the recommendations they will make to the central committee.

There is still another mile to go! The Commission continues to wrestle with one issue: common prayer. There is an awareness that solutions to institutional matters, such as membership and procedures of vot-

ing, do not make sense as long as the spiritual questions of why and how we are joined together as churches remain unanswered.

Deliberations are not easy. Feelings are stirred up. Indeed, prayer comes from and penetrates to the deepest core of each participant. The discussion is very frank, but sometimes this openness hurts people. Under such circumstances neither speaking nor listening is easy.

The Commission discusses carefully prepared theological and practical guidelines for common prayer. For some of its members this is real progress. The imperative of common prayer is affirmed and clarity is brought as to how prayer services should be prepared in the future. For

Consecration of the village church of Dumbrava near Iasi, Romania, October 2000.

The Easter liturgy is celebrated in the church of the Saviour of All Nations, Shoushi, Nagorno-Karabagh.

36

Consensus decision-making

From the World Council's inception, decision-making in the governing bodies has been based on the Anglo-Saxon model of parliamentary debate and majority voting which is common in many Protestant churches but alien to other traditions and cultures.

The Special Commission opted for consensus decision-making, which allows for diverse opinions to be expressed, and seeks to reach a "common mind" of the assembly before decisions are finalized. Agreed procedures regulate the way meetings are organized, and the method will not be used, for example, for administrative decisions.

Membership and representation

The work of the Special Commission on membership was accompanied by a separate membership study group appointed by the executive committee. Both the Commission and the study group made recommendations on how to recognize various levels of relationship with the WCC (see p. 20).

The central committee established a 14-member Permanent Committee on Consensus and Collaboration, which reports to the executive and central committees, to oversee and assist the implementation of the Special Commission's recommendations.

The proposals have been further discussed and tested during the period leading to the ninth assembly, and member churches and ecumenical

others, this is a step back. A number of questions do not receive full or fully satisfactory responses. The overall tone of the document follows the line of "discipline" rather than of spiritual freedom and joy. All agree, however, that the guidelines try to raise awareness about the ways in which we might unintentionally offend each other and strive to make planners of common prayer more aware of potential areas of concern.

After the end of the session, members of the Commission attend vespers in the Lutheran cathedral in Helsinki. The service is led jointly by the Lutheran and Orthodox bishops of Helsinki. As the long evening settles over Finland, the bishops and congregation follow the foremost of their agreed guidelines:

"We must pray together."

partners of the WCC have been invited to study carefully and respond to the proposals made in the final report.

The Special Commission has not simply been a process of making structural changes to the WCC. The members of the Commission have spoken of the transformation and recommitment they went through personally and as a group during their three years of intense work. What began as discussion between two potentially divided groups became a mutual journey to solve common concerns. The process has demonstrated a new level of dialogue and engagement among different traditions. The

Special Commission has become an invitation and a model to churches in the ecumenical movement to use the space offered by the WCC to grapple with central issues in our life and witness together as a fellowship of churches.

The relationships described in this chapter are primarily the responsibility of the Church and Ecumenical Relations staff team.

The choir practises in the Pentecostal church of Mare Rouge, Haiti.

Building the
Unity of the Church

As millions join in a Week of Prayer for Christian Unity each year, recent efforts affirm that true unity is built on understanding fundamental issues of faith and how it is practised – such as baptism, peace, and the nature and mission of the church. At the same time, Christians learn how to create safe spaces for dialogue on dividing issues, and to shape church and community life so that all may contribute fully.

Children worship in the Good Hope Lutheran church of Kuala Lumpur, Malaysia, August 2004.

Issues of ecclesiology, theology and spirituality are central to the life and work of the WCC – who we are, what we believe and how we worship as churches and people of faith. Thus a central part of the work of the WCC is bringing together theologians, teachers, ordained and lay leaders from all Christian traditions to reflect together on the sources of Christian unity and division.

Considerable progress has been made during this period in all the study areas approved by the WCC assembly and central committee. Many of the issues come out of continuing reflection and response from

a pivotal study, *Baptism, Eucharist and Ministry,* finalized in Lima, Peru, in 1982.

Study, as a distinct methodology, involves extensive reflection, consultation, drafting, discussion of texts, redrafting. Such processes may take many years, but final texts are brought forward only when sufficient agreement has been reached. Thus the process itself is critical to the search for unity, and the final outcomes are valuable to both churches and academic institutions.

Accompanying such studies are practical efforts in church-union discussions and encouraging expressions of unity in worship and spiritual life.

Studies towards unity

Studies on the sources — both theological and social — of the unity and division of the churches are undertaken by the Faith and Order Commission, the world's most representative official theological forum for Christian unity.

With 120 members representing the WCC member churches and several non-member churches, notably the Roman Catholic Church, the Commission discusses theological issues touching on the way different traditions conceive the Christian faith, and the way in which they organize their own lives and their life together. The Commission also studies social, cultural, political, racial and other factors as they affect the unity of the church.

The full Plenary Commission normally meets once between assemblies. It last met in August 2004 in Kuala Lumpur, Malaysia — the first time it gathered in a majority Muslim country. The context of the meeting proved particularly significant in witnessing and discussing the unity of the church in the midst of the religious plurality that increasingly

39

Children involved in a church outreach programme in Tondegesan, west of Manado, North Sulawesi, Indonesia.

marks the world in which we live. The Commission examined the progress of its studies and proposed guidelines for further work.

Drawing on the Plenary Commission's comments, texts from each Faith and Order study were revised for presentation to the standing commission meeting in Crete in June 2005. At this its last meeting, this standing commission reviewed all the work done under its mandate since the Harare assembly. It was a moment of self-evaluation and accountability to the churches, but also a time to look forward to the next stage of Faith and Order work. As a result, the text reflecting the present stage of the study on the church – entitled "The Nature and Mission of the Church" – will be sent to the churches for consideration and appropriate response. Other texts, reflecting studies which have finished their work, will be

shared with the churches for local use. In some areas of study, work remains to be done and here proposals were offered for consideration by the next standing commission and WCC governing bodies.

The range of studies has meant different programme areas of the Council – including Mission and Evangelism; Justice, Peace and Creation; and Inter-Religious Dialogue – have been involved, and there has been a greater involvement of young theologians.

The study on "The Nature and Purpose of the Church" focuses on ecclesiology – the understanding of what it means to be church. The goal of the study is a common statement reflecting what the churches can say together about the church. A draft text was developed and sent in 1998 to the churches, theological commis-

Faith and Order plenary commission, August 2004. Archbishop John Onaiyekan of the Catholic church, Nigeria (left), and Metropolitan Bishoy of Damietta, Coptic Orthodox church of Egypt.

sions and councils of churches for their reactions.

While responses were incorporated into new drafts, efforts were made to address confessional and regional imbalances by getting further input from different parts of the world and from Orthodox churches. At the same time, several consultations helped to clarify specific themes, such as "Authority and Authoritative Teaching" and "Ministry and Ordination in the Community of Women and Men in the Church". Reports from the consultations have been published.

The central committee in August 2002, in addition to plenaries on baptism and ecclesiology, received the final report of the Special Commission on Orthodox Participation in the WCC. With the report came the recommendation

for further work on specific ecclesiological questions.

The central committee requested Faith and Order to prepare a concise statement on ecclesiology for discussion at the ninth assembly. The statement should take into account especially the relation between the church as local community and universal reality, and the fact that the church is both diverse and one. The statement was developed through a broadly consultative process involving the central committee and the Special Commission as well as Faith and Order.

The study on "Ethnic Identity, National Identity and the Search for Unity" recognizes that the life and witness of the churches are impaired by their divisions, tragically – and often most intractably – when these follow lines of ethnic or national

41

Opening worship for the WCC central committee, Potsdam, 2001.

Elements of worship: the liturgy of the Orthodox church in Poland is celebrated.

identities in conflict. Through this study the WCC has been looking more closely at Christian unity in local contexts, particularly in situations of conflict.

Most recently, the WCC has been encouraging local reflection and soliciting reactions to material produced from consultations of biblical scholars, theologians and social scientists held in 2003 and 2004, together with self-studies from Sudan and Fiji. Responses allow the WCC to develop materials for churches in conflict situations, to help them reflect on their role in maintaining or legitimizing divisions both in church and society, and on their calling to witness together to reconciliation and justice.

Baptism is fundamental to Christian faith, and the mutual recognition of baptism is considered to be one basis of the modern ecumenical movement. Baptism is into the one body of Christ, not into one part of the body of Christ. In recognizing another church's baptism, a church acknowledges that Christ has acted, through that church, to incorporate a person into his one body. Therefore, the mutual recognition of baptism raises the wider question of the mutual recognition of the churches themselves.

While the 1982 document *Baptism, Eucharist and Ministry* revealed a remarkable degree of agreement on the subject, it was clear that more work needed to be done.

The central committee in early 2001 directly addressed the question of baptism, noting its centrality to the work of the Joint Working Group between the Roman Catholic Church and the WCC, as well as dialogue with Evangelicals and Pentecostals. The committee requested that member churches reflect "on the meaning and significance of baptism for their participation in the ecumenical fellowship".

The resulting statement, "One Baptism: Towards Mutual Recognition of Christian Initiation", was drafted in 2001 and entered a process of reflection and revision on the basis of responses from the Commission as well as from churches, theologians, liturgists and others. The document aims to clarify what the mutual recognition of baptism means, to explain some of its implications, and to identify issues preventing mutual recognition. It looks at biblical texts, sacraments, baptismal practice, the church and church membership, and suggests ways of moving forward – including practical ways of expressing recognition.

A collection of baptismal liturgies with commentaries provided by the respective churches is also being produced as a contribution to the churches' discussion of the understanding, practice and mutual recognition of baptism. Through this work the WCC hopes to build a greater degree of mutual recognition, and to encourage progress on issues which hinder that recognition.

Baptism in the Church of Melanesia, Honiara, Solomon Islands.

The Harare assembly requested a study on theological anthropology – the understanding of the nature of the human person from a Christian point of view, and its implications for issues such as community identity, human sexuality, disabilities or bio-ethics.

A series of consultations focused on the nature of the human person made in the image of God, especially in light of the challenges to the understanding of human identity coming from current social and scientific developments. The resulting text, published in 2005, proposes "Ten Common Affirmations" as a basis for the churches' common reflection and action on a wide range of issues which turn on the understanding of human nature.

Relevant to all the studies is ecumenical hermeneutics – the way in which the texts, symbols and practices of different Christian churches may be interpreted, communicated and received. Reports and papers from key consultations on hermeneutics were compiled in 2005 to help churches clarify their own distinctive approach to the interpretation of scripture and encourage them to pursue an ecumenical approach to scripture, tradition and experience.

Theological reflection on peace

Out of the Decade to Overcome Violence, a study process was begun on "Nurturing Peace, Overcoming Violence: In the Way of Christ for the Sake of the World". Churches, seminaries and ecumenical partners have been invited to reflect on major themes of justice, peace and reconciliation.

In addition to inviting reflection and input on study documents from indi-

Baptism in the Good Hope Lutheran church, Kuala Lumpur, Malaysia.

vidual churches and institutions, consultations held in different regions spark focused reflection from specific contexts. A consultation on the theme of "Affirming Human Dignity, Rights of the Peoples and the Integrity of Creation" was held in Rwanda in December 2004, and a smaller one on "Realizing Mutuality and Interdependence in a World of Diverse Identities" was held in Norway in April 2005.

One of the themes, "Interrogating and Redefining Power", was the focus of two key consultations. One, in December 2003, was held cooperatively by Faith and Order, International Affairs, and Justice, Peace, Creation which integrated theological questions of peace and justice with questions and challenges around the churches' work with the United Nations, and on issues such as impunity and reconciliation, economic globalization, climate change and violence against women. Younger theologians from the South then met in Chiang Mai in February 2004 for spirited discussions exploring their distinct perspectives on power as persons whose theology is shaped in contexts of intense struggles for life, justice and liberation.

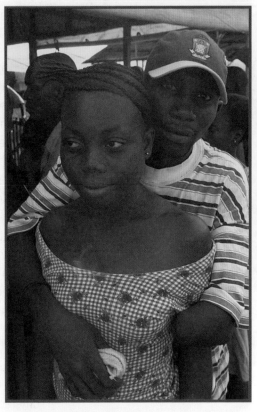

A young woman and her boyfriend at the Freetown shelter for amputees and their families established as a result of the civil war in Sierra Leone.

A core group of theologians has accompanied the process and will develop the resulting material into a publication.

Human sexuality

While issues about sexuality were not officially on the agenda of the Harare assembly, controversies and debates reflecting the vast range of policy and practice, particularly on the issue of homosexuality, simmered under the surface. Recognizing the potential for division within and

The church is by definition a place and a process of communion, open to and inviting all people without discrimination. It is a place of hospitality and a place of welcome, in the manner that Abraham and Sarah received God's messengers in the Old Testament (Gen. 18). It is an earthly reflection of a divine unity that is at the same time worshipped as Trinity. It is a community of people with different yet complementary gifts. It is a vision of wholeness as well as of healing, of caring and of sharing at once.

Just as the body is one and has many members, so it is with Christ (1 Cor. 12:12).

45

We all accept and proclaim that this is what the church is and stands for. It is the basis of our unity as Christians. Then why is it that, all too often, certain people among us and around us (usually those whom we consider as being unfamiliar or as strangers, as different or perhaps disabled) are marginalized and even excluded? Wherever this happens, even by passive omission, the church is not being what it is called to become. The church is denying its own reality. In the church, we are called to act differently.

*From "**A Church of All and for All: An Interim Statement**"*

Mitä sinä teet 1. joulukuuta?

Vad gör du den 1. december?

"Equal light on you and me" – from a poster competition promoting ecumenical advocacy. Artist: Kari Tuhkanen, Finland.

46

Participants in the consultation agreed that a model of unity, if it is to deserve such a label, must be tangible enough to make a witness to the world, intense enough that those in it recognize their responsibility for one another, costly enough that churches are changed as a result of being in it, and intentional enough that the body of Christ is renewed through the sharing of gifts. We also agree, however, that no one model guarantees (or denies) such an outcome. The new models remind us to look for partners in unexpected places and to expect to be surprised by what God will do in our midst.

Seventh International Consultation of United and Uniting Churches

Driebergen, The Netherlands, September 2002

among churches, the programme guidelines committee asked for a study and dialogue on the theological, social and cultural aspects of human sexuality.

In response, the WCC general secretary invited a number of representatives from member churches to form a reference group on human sexuality. The reference group reviewed and analyzed eighty church statements on all aspects of human sexuality, as well as a congregational study guide prepared by the Anglican diocese of Johannesburg, South Africa. Members facilitated regional seminars on biblical texts in 2003 in the Caribbean, Europe, Fiji, India, Kenya, Latin America, Lebanon and North America.

The general secretary also appointed a human sexuality staff group within the WCC to relate to the reference group, linking the issue of human sexuality to WCC programme areas

such as HIV/AIDS and the study on theological anthropology.

The two groups organized three seminars at the Ecumenical Institute at Bossey. The first invited participants from different cultures to share their perspectives on sexuality, the second analyzed church statements on the subject, and the third focused on Bible studies.

The October 2004 issue of *The Ecumenical Review* focused on sexuality. In addition, a Risk book was published in 2005 to encourage and facilitate discussion in the churches and by the central committee.

The multi-faceted process highlighted the diversity of contexts and the different issues that are of concern for the churches in different regions. Issues that have come to the forefront include HIV and AIDS, violence against women and sexual abuse of children, breakdown of the family, homosexuality and the diverse understandings of "the image of God".

The process has also emphasized the fact that in dealing with such potentially divisive issues, attempts to mainstream particular positions or produce authoritative statements only deepen division within and among churches. Ecumenical spaces continue to be needed to enable encounter, analysis, dialogue, education and a pastoral approach to the issues at stake.

"A Church of All and for All"

An interim theological statement, which stimulates conversation with persons with disabilities, was presented to the central committee in 2003. The statement emphasizes the acceptance of all persons as made in the image of God and the inter-relatedness of persons. It makes important distinctions between healing and cure and challenges the assumption that disability and sin are correlated. Expressing the gifts, insights and perceptions which persons with disabilities can offer, it calls on the church to become more inclusive, theologically and physically, especially in relation to worship.

Supporting United and Uniting churches

United churches are those formed from unions across or within confessional families. Uniting churches are those moving towards union, whether through integrating ecclesial structures or entering covenant relationships of different kinds.

The seventh international consultation of United and Uniting churches was held in the Netherlands in 2002. Participants explored the inter-relation of unity, mission and identity through presentations, case studies and reports from unions and union processes around the world, workshops on theological and practical issues facing the churches today, and intensive encounters with *Samen op Weg* (Together on the Way), the church-union process in the Netherlands which hosted the meeting – and led in 2004 to the formation of a new United church, the Protestant Church in the Netherlands.

Since the sixth consultation of United and Uniting churches in 1995, other steps towards union include the formation of the racially mixed Uniting Presbyterian Church in Southern

Left: Pro Educatione is a school for children with relatively minor physical and mental disabilities, Brasov, Romania. Right: Basketball practice at the eighth assembly in Harare.

47

"The ecumenical movement in the 21st century is challenged to respond to the spiritual yearning of our time and especially the spirituality being sought by the younger generation. Ecumenism must relate organically to this yearning for more experiential dimensions of faith."

Rev. Dr Samuel Kobia, *in his message to the 2005 central committee*

Chiara Lubich, founder of the Focolare movement, with Konrad Raiser. She addressed a plenary in Geneva on "a spirituality of communion" during a visit to the WCC.

Africa (1999); the commitment to create the Communion of Churches in India, signifying an even closer bond of shared confession, witness and service among the Church of North India, the Church of South India, and the Mar Thoma Church (1999); the union of the United Reformed Church in the United Kingdom and the Congregational Union of Scotland (2000); and the inauguration of a substantive covenant among nine US denominations, known as Churches Uniting in Christ (2002). Reports on church-union developments were published in *The Ecumenical Review* in July 2002 and a further account, to reflect progress since 2002, is in preparation.

Worship and spirituality

The WCC helps educate worship leaders and provides space for the exchange of worship resources by churches throughout the world. Materials for common prayer and worship have been prepared for ecumenical events and for churches themselves as they seek to go beyond their own cultural and liturgical traditions. A series of worship workshops has been organized, and a worship resource centre encourages sharing of resources among churches, and looks at the ways in which they have built up a tradition of praying together.

The Ecumenical Prayer Cycle has been revised and published and distributed recently, enabling local churches to journey systematically in prayer together through every region of the world and through every week of the year.

The WCC has also engaged more directly in dialogue with communities of renewal such as the Focolare movement for spiritual and social

Father Pishoy Musungu leads morning prayer in the St Abanoub Coptic Orthodox church near Kisumu, Kenya.

renewal, and the communities of St Egidio, Iona and Chemin Neuf. A visit to the WCC in 2002 by Chiara Lubich, founder of the Focolare, evoked the "spirituality of unity" as central for a renewed hope for a common ecumenical journey.

The WCC also continues long-term dialogue seeking ways towards a common celebration of Easter among churches following different traditions and calendars.

Week of Prayer for Christian Unity

Every year, thousands of churches and communities all over the world join in reaffirming their commitment to Christian unity in the face of today's social, political and economic divisions.

The Week of Prayer for Christian Unity can trace its inspiration back to the second half of the 18th century, but it was not until 1966 that the WCC's Faith and Order Commission and the Pontifical Council for Promoting Christian Unity began their official joint preparation of the Week of Prayer material. The material for the 2005 Week of Prayer was, for the first time, not only prepared but also published jointly by the WCC and the Roman Catholic Church.

The initial draft of the material is drawn up each year by a local ecu-

WCC central committee moderator His Holiness Aram I, member Archbishop Anastasios of Tirana, Durrës and All Albania, Rev. Dr Konrad Raiser and Rev. Dr Alan Falconer at the service in Lausanne cathedral, Switzerland, to commemorate the 75th anniversary of the first conference on Faith and Order, August 2002.

49

Anastasia Vassiliadou, Church of Greece, makes a presentation at the 75th anniversary of Faith and Order, Lausanne university, Switzerland, August 2002.

menical group and is rooted in the challenges facing the churches in their search for unity in that particular context. A biblical passage is selected for each year that speaks to an issue of immediate relevance for the churches in our contemporary world.

The Week of Prayer for Christian Unity is traditionally celebrated 18-25 January in the northern hemisphere; in the southern hemisphere other dates are sometimes chosen, in some cases around Pentecost.

75th anniversary of efforts towards visible unity

The 75th anniversary of Faith and Order was held in August 2002 in Lausanne, site of the first world conference on Faith and Order in 1927. An ecumenical service in the cathedral was preceded by speeches reflecting on the history and hopes of the search for visible unity. To sustained applause, Anastasia Vassiliadou from the Church of Greece, at the time a youth intern at the WCC, expressed the essence of the ecumenical movement: "God wills unity, not for the sake of the church but for the sake of the world; and we constantly pray to God: Your will be done."

The activities described in this chapter are the primary responsibility of the Faith and Order staff team.

Witnessing to the World

The 13th world mission conference, held in Athens in May 2005, brought together the most diverse group of Christian traditions ever to celebrate and challenge each other on mission, reconciliation and mutual accountability. The scourge of HIV and AIDS requires new understandings of mission and service and, as through the Ecumenical HIV/AIDS Initiative in Africa, the development and sharing of expertise and care.

Sharing the faith in word and deed is central to the Christian calling. Yet this common calling which unites Christians in spirit often seems to divide churches in practice. When compared to its intention – to bring the "good news" that promises "life in all its fullness" – many in the ecumenical movement will confess that Christians not only often fall woefully short, but practices on the ground can become a counter-witness to what is preached.

"Mission", the Harare assembly programme guidelines committee emphasized from the first round of hearings, "should be kept at the centre of the ecumenical movement, and must be held together with the concern for unity."

The underlying vision for the WCC's work on Christian witness is ecumenical evangelism, or mission in unity. The WCC, through study, train-

A procession makes its way to opening prayer at the Athens world mission conference, 2005.

> There is the common conviction that central to the work of Christian unity is an urgent need for all Christians to be able to give a truly common witness to the whole Christian faith.
>
> **Seventh Report of the Joint Working Group**
> between the Roman Catholic Church and the WCC

In ecumenical reflection and work, important distinctions regarding mission, evangelism and proselytism have been made. Mission *carries "a holistic understanding" that the proclamation of the good news of the gospel comes by word, deeds and worship – and indeed, by the everyday witness and teaching that strengthen people's faith and actions in community and with God.* Evangelism *refers more specifically to the intentional "voicing of the gospel, including the invitation to personal conversion to a new life in Christ and to discipleship".* Proselytism *is to be distinguished from mission and evangelism and describes efforts by Christians who try to win "converts" from other Christian communities, often taking advantage of the vulnerabilities of peoples and cultures.*

Edited summary of WCC definitions as they appear in "Mission and Evangelism in Unity today", the study document adopted in 2000 by the Commission on World Mission and Evangelism. The quotations are from the document.

ing and practical effort, searches for ways different churches can witness together "so that the world may believe" (John 17:21). The goal is not some "unrealistic super-church ecclesiology" nor simply avoiding a sense of competition or rivalry among churches. The aim is to witness truly to the common faith through Jesus Christ and demonstrate the message of unity found in the gospel through the ways Christians live in their communities.

Since the Edinburgh world mission conference in 1910, this goal has remained constant although in many ways the world has become more complex – culturally, economically and politically. Thus marking

"progress" towards the goal can prove difficult when understandings reached in one area find new challenges and setbacks in another.

A number of achievements have taken place in the period since Harare, however. For the first time Roman Catholics, and representatives from Pentecostal and Evangelical groups, are full members of the Commission on World Mission and Evangelism (CWME). The world mission conference in Athens may well have been the most diverse and representative to date with strong involvement of Evangelicals, Pentecostals and Roman Catholics. Consultations within the WCC fellowship and with mission bodies and

Delegates break for small group discussions at the CWME in Athens, 2005.

networks of the wider constituency have shown on which points there is agreement on the approach to mission, on which work must continue to resolve conflictual theological issues, and where deep wounds still prevent witness in unity.

Reflecting on mission today

The Harare assembly's programme guidelines committee posed a key question for reflection by the WCC fellowship: How do we as churches engage together in mission and evangelism in the midst of a highly pluralistic world?

The WCC has approached the question through providing space for churches and mission partners within and outside of the WCC fellowship to reflect on theology and experience, to dialogue and to draft statements and study documents. Consultations serve to test ideas and highlight trends and challenges, assess partnerships and encourage exploration of new models of mission work. Study documents not only help all those in dialogue to continue to reflect and move forward in the quest for *mission in unity*, but also serve to teach and inspire those in mission on the ground.

The Commission on World Mission and Evangelism (CWME) adopted in 2000 the study document "Mission and Evangelism in Unity Today" that

In short, churches and mission organizations should develop a theology of the fullness of life that puts fullness, salvation and reconciliation into relation with our mission as healing communities.

Report of missiology conference,
London, April 2002

The funeral of the abbot of Neamt monastery in southern Bucovina, Romania.

53

The testimonies that we have heard in this consultation confirm our belief that God's activity is not limited to the body but has to do with the salvation of people as whole persons and with transforming relationships in the family and in society. These real-life stories have encouraged us to continue in prayer for divine healing in the broken bodies of men and women suffering from various diseases and even in extreme situations. They have inspired us to encourage those with various gifts in our congregations to be involved in all these healing processes through a combination of medical care, pastoral psychological support and the ministry of prayer.

Pastoral letter to the churches *from the WCC-CLAI Chile consultation on faith, healing and mission, 2003*

summarizes developments since the 1982 statement, which remains the official WCC position on mission. The study document was one of the key reflection resources for the world mission conference in 2005.

In London in 2002, a major consultation on missiology brought together delegates and consultants from key mission bodies to address changing identities in a pluralistic world. Co-organized by CWME, the Council for World Mission, Cevaa – Community of Churches in Mission, and the United Evangelical Mission, the consultation also focused on the dialogue needed with Pentecostal and charismatic Christians on approaches to health, healing and faith; the challenge HIV and AIDS poses to mission and ecclesiology; and new models of partnership in mission worldwide.

A focus on faith and healing is one of the outcomes of dialogue with those in the Pentecostal and charismatic traditions. An earlier consultation in 2000 held in cooperation with the Mission Academy of Hamburg, Germany, brought around forty missiologists, mission practitioners and medical personnel to take stock of the present emphasis on faith and healing in missiology, intercultural dialogue and medicine. Participants listened to individual and community experiences of healing in different cultures, and identified urgent needs for future research and ecumenical dialogue or action.

These consultations led to international and regional encounters on faith, healing and mission (Ghana 2002, Chile 2003) which continued to address the diversity of issues involved, from approaches to suffering and healing in different cultures and Christian traditions, to interpretations of exorcism and the influence of the world of spirits. The participants, half of whom came from Pentecostal charismatic churches and half from ecumenical "mainline" churches, were able to increase their mutual understandings of different traditions and build trust for further discussion.

The latest consultation in the series was held in November 2004 in India, as an Afro-Asian preparatory meeting for the Athens conference. Organized in cooperation with the AACC and the CCA, it focused on the relation between mission, power and a holistic understanding of healing and reconciliation.

The need was felt to provide a synthesis of recent insights and results from these missiological processes. A 2004 seminar prepared a statement on a renewed approach to pneumatology – the study of the Holy Spirit – and the interface between mission and reconciliation. Revised by the CWME Commission, it became, together with a second statement on mission and healing produced at the end of 2004, one of the main preparatory documents for the world mission conference.

While most consultations aim to bring a diversity of people to the space for dialogue and reflection, some others are designed to give specific perspectives. Thus, for example, women from churches, movements, theological colleges and mission agencies were brought together through a series of meetings to focus on experiences of women in the missionary tasks of the church, assist leadership development and affirm the contributions of women to the mission of the church. Young missiologists also gathered in early 2005 to address pneumatology and mission under the theme of the mission conference.

The Harare assembly suggested continued follow-up to the gospel-and-cultures study, which led to dialogue and study on how identities are formed, pluralism, and multicultural ministry. A consultation brought together in 2002 more than fifty representatives from gospel-and-cultures networks from various continents to address the central issue of mission in secular and post-modern contexts. A series of forums on muliticultural ministry held in Australia and Thailand focused on

Left: Ecumenical marchers at the 2003 World Social Forum. Centre: Pastor Fermin Siñani has led the Evangelical Lutheran congregation of Calasaya, Bolivia, since founding it in 1969. Right: A traditional Malaysian dance group at the Faith and Order plenary, Kuala Lumpur, July 2004.

55

The fellowship and community that we experienced during our school became for us a sign of the unity that we already have, and further encouraged us to pursue a deepening of our visible unity for the sake of the mission of God to the world. We, as individuals and churches, commit ourselves to the work of fulfilling his great commission in our church, our nation and our region. It is in the Spirit that we greet you and invite you to further engage in mission and evangelism together.

Letter to Churches,
Fiji, November 2004

practices and stories of how to approach multicultural ministry and mission.

To respond to a real need as well as a concern expressed in the Harare programme guidelines report, a study process was launched in common by staff and scholars linked to the three WCC networks Mission and Evangelism, Faith and Order and Inter-religious Relations, to produce a draft study text on a theological approach to religious plurality, which would serve as a background document for interested persons and churches. This, as well as another common consultation between Faith and Order and Mission and Evangelism on "ecclesiology and mission", show the increasing cooperation between different streams of the ecumenical movement on important contemporary theological issues.

To promote and demonstrate mission in unity, as well as maximize resources and expertise, the WCC also works with numerous mission organizations and networks, seeking joint cooperation in projects wherever possible.

The study documents, issues of dialogue and outcomes of consultations are published by the WCC in the quarterly *International Review of Mission* (IRM), which is the oldest existing ecumenical and international journal on mission.

An offering of gifts at the opening service of the WCC's eighth assembly, Harare, December 1998.

Learning how to do mission in unity

The WCC maintains its commitment to common witness through training leaders in evangelism and creating safe places for the poor and marginalized to reflect and act together and inform the wider church of what it means to be in solidarity with the poor and how people can be empowered for witness and transformation.

Schools of evangelism expose participants to different cultural contexts and traditions in addition to building their skills in ecumenical evangelism. Since Harare, schools have been held in Asia (India), the Caribbean (Cuba), Eastern Europe (Poland), the Middle East (Syria) and the Pacific (Fiji). Each location carries important lessons, such as: What does it mean to share the "good news" in a religiously pluralistic society, with competing secular forces, in a society already dominantly Christian, in the birthplace of Christianity itself?

Increasingly, the schools are seen as "trainings for trainers" with the hope that participants will go back to their communities and influence others to share the good news of the gospel in collaboration rather than competition.

The schools are open to people outside of the WCC fellowship, bringing people united in their passion to share the gospel. Roman Catholic

One example of URM in action is through the ACAPES centre in Senegal, part of the URM network, which was formed as an alternative school with volunteer teachers when many students were dismissed after a school crisis in the country. The centre has grown to offer a variety of courses to those who, for whatever reason, cannot finish school. The centre also supports women, men and youth movements.

During the URM global working group meeting held in Senegal in 2001, hosted by ACAPES, the (cont. on page 58)

57

A market in Munda, New George Island, Solomon Islands.

(cont. from page 57) working group was informed that, for the exposure visit that is always part of the meeting, they would need to visit the south to demonstrate their solidarity with the people in the midst of the violent conflict there. At the airport, they were met by 1000 young people, and ended up leading a march for peace. They met government officials, and then the leader of the rebel group, who at that time was under house arrest. To them, he said that in no way can anyone justify violence. Two weeks later, the rebel leader, for the first time, agreed to talk to the government, which was the beginning of the peace process.

The local people told URM that the visit of the working group was one factor, along with the youth movements, that helped to crystallize the peace efforts.

participants are active, as well as Protestants and Orthodox.

One step in this direction came in the school for evangelism held in November 2004 in the Pacific in which the widest range of mission workers gathered to discuss proselytism, inter-religious dialogue and common witness. This is an important step in the process of creating space for trust and dialogue as a basis for further action.

The *Ecumenical Letter on Evangelism* was redesigned and is published in English, French, German and Spanish. It provides a personal and supportive approach to those engaged in mission and evangelism on the ground.

Urban Rural Mission (URM) challenges thinking and practice that separate social ministry from evangelism. URM approaches mission and evangelism from the perspective of the poor and marginalized – communities often on the receiving end of classical evangelistic efforts, but which in ecumenical perspectives are considered as main actors within God's mission.

Regional URM networks support community organizing at the grassroots, facilitating education and small income-producing projects that help raise communities' standard of living as well as awareness of and involvement in issues affecting people's community and country so that they can, for themselves, see the root

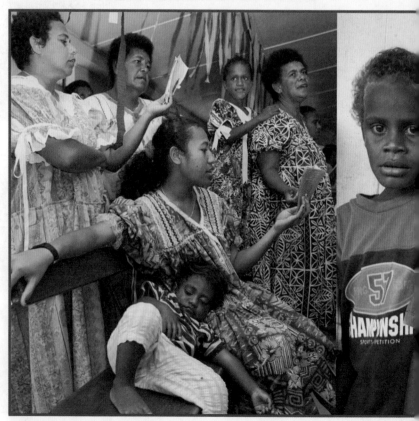

causes of problems they face and are able to act on them. A global working group enables cross-regional exchanges.

"Mission from the perspective of people in struggle", the theme of URM since 2002, promotes concrete ways the churches can help challenge structures of injustice from the perspective of the marginalized. The movement aims to link urban and rural community organizations, people's movements and networks together with churches and mission bodies to demonstrate that the poor no longer expect the church to help them, but to be with them, learn from them to name what is wrong, and cooperate with them in challenging the systems for fundamental change. For URM this is at the core of what Christian mission is all about.

In 2004, all regionally organized URM networks met in Ghana for an intercontinental major missiological consultation to share the results of the work done on the common theme since 2002 and provide the perspective of people in struggle to an understanding of mission as healing and reconciliation. In the words of their final declaration, "mission will lead to healing and reconciliation when it is characterized by a spiritual discipline that resists egoism and oppression and breaks the yoke of injustice".

Left: Sunday worship in the Presbyterian church of Imere, on the outskirts of Port Vila, Vanuatu. Centre: Children at the Florence Young Christian School, Honiara, Solomon Islands. Right: An Afghan woman refugee in Pakistan sews a quilt as part of an income-generating project run by Church World Service and ACT International in Quetta, Pakistan.

59

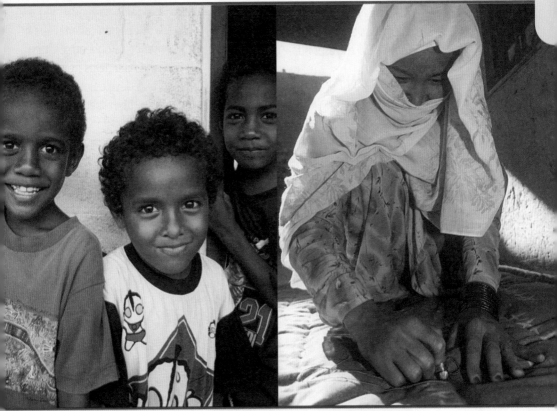

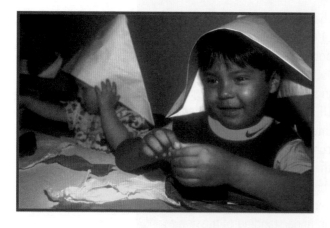

Above: A daycare centre in Armenia, Colombia, responded to the needs of homeless families following the January 1999 earthquake. ACT member organizations including the Methodist Church of Colombia provided essential assistance.

Below, left: A poster encouraging ecumenical advocacy and action on HIV/AIDS. Artist: Babatunde Morgan, Sierra Leone.

Below, right: Kamwokya Christian Caring community health centre in Kampala offers HIV/AIDS tests at reasonable rates.

The churches' health and healing ministry

Health is also a focus in WCC mission efforts, not only because health care represents one of the churches' traditionally strong areas of mission (in particular due to the work of the Christian Medical Commission from 1968 to 1991) but because the HIV/AIDS pandemic is one of the critical issues of our time to which the church as a whole must continue to learn how to respond.

In addition to dialogue and study on aspects of faith and healing, the WCC promotes practical efforts to strengthen health education, provide sustainable resources for disease

prevention and cure, and advocate and support proper care at all levels of need, particularly in response to HIV and AIDS. The WCC also advocates equitable sharing and rational investment in drugs and medical equipment, particularly through the work of the Ecumenical Pharmaceutical Network.

The WCC works with Christian health networks to enable them to reflect on their approaches to primary health care, HIV/AIDS prevention programmes and the growing role of church-related health-care facilities and workers in post-conflict situations. Other efforts, such as workshops in North Asia and the Caribbean, for instance, assist in the incorporation of HIV/AIDS in the curriculum of theological institutions. Establishing and strengthening a network of ecumenical enablers in Latin America/Caribbean, Eastern Europe and Asia helps in resourcing, training and developing policy with churches in the respective regions.

Contact, the ecumenical journal of health-related issues available in sev-

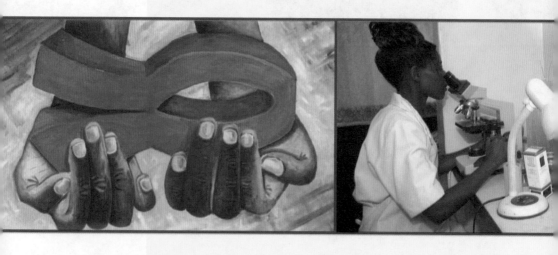

eral languages, continues to be a valuable resource. In 2003 it became an on-line magazine that could be downloaded and reprinted locally in order to take advantage of new technology and the vast Christian health networks while being cost-effective. The WCC carries out an important networking function, linking church-related people active in health care with other concerned organizations and networks, including those willing to provide resources. The WCC continues to provide a key networking role among grassroots health movements, regional ecumenical church-related health associations and networks, and international platforms such as the NGO Forum for Health, WHO and UNICEF.
(See also Churches respond to HIV and AIDS p. 65)

Conference on world mission and evangelism

The world mission and evangelism conference held in Athens in May 2005, on the theme "Come, Holy Spirit, Heal and Reconcile! Called in Christ to Be Reconciling and Healing Communities", was the 13th in the

line of such conferences since the Edinburgh world mission conference of 1910, generally seen as the quickening point of the modern ecumenical movement.

One marker in the progress of ecumenical work dedicated to mission and evangelism may be seen in the development of the conferences themselves. Edinburgh, which was a great step forward in cooperation among Protestant mission councils, had no Catholic or Orthodox delegates, and only about 1 percent of the 1400 participants came from what would later be termed the "third world". Orthodox churches became key actors in facets of the ecumenical movement by the 1920s, but Catholic participation was not possible until the Second Vatican Council.

Participation in the world mission conferences has expanded greatly, in particular since the middle of the 20th century, and the 2005 event was one of the most universal mission gatherings ever. Approximately one-quarter of the six hundred participants came from Evangelical,

Below: Worship in the Church of Melanesia in Honiara, Solomon Islands.

A cross of olive wood arrives at the Athens 2005 CWME. A gift of Jerusalem churches, it was made from trees in Palestine uprooted in building Israel's separation barrier.

Pentecostal and Roman Catholic backgrounds, including the 42 Catholic delegates who attended for the first time as full voting members. It was also the first world mission conference to be held in a majority Orthodox country. The participants came from all continents and included young people, women and men involved in Christian witness as church and mission leaders, theologians and missiologists.

A youth pre-conference and stewards orientation programme held during the week prior to the Athens conference helped prepare younger participants to make their contribution to the proceedings. Nevertheless, the total number of youth participants was disappointing, and a strong appeal was received from youth delegates and stewards calling on the World Council of Churches and the ecumenical movement at large to become more intentional in ensuring

that target numbers for youth participation are achieved at the ninth assembly and subsequent events.

The conference was designed to encourage the spiritual life of the gathered Christians, and to build a sense of community. Time was allotted for common prayer, Bible study and "home-group" discussions of matters relating to the conference. In the tent where the conference met for morning and evening prayer, a five-metre cross stood as a striking symbol. On the first morning of the conference, a small boat delivered the cross as a gift from the churches of Jerusalem. The cross is formed from pieces of wood gleaned from olive trees that were uprooted in and near Bethlehem as the Israeli government built its wall of separation on Palestinian land.

Plenary sessions at the Athens conference allowed occasions for signifi-

cant presentations on themes related to mission, healing and reconciliation: the building of community in an age of fragmentation, principles and practices of overcoming violence, economic globalization, HIV/AIDS and stigmatization. In addition to plenary presentations and home-group discussion, market-places of ideas and experience bearing the Greek name *synaxeis* provided opportunities to raise issues that had not appeared on the formal agenda.

The studies and activities throughout the conference provided the basis for preparation and reflection. By the end of the conference, it could be seen that several central themes had emerged from the dialogue there; the following were among them:

- An expanding constellation of Orthodox, Protestant, Pentecostal, Catholic and other participants signals the evolution of relationships among Christians of diverse

backgrounds; this holds tremendous potential for the future, even as it raises questions and challenges for all concerned.

- A mid-point review of the Decade to Overcome Violence helped to discern how the WCC's mission networks have affected and been affected by the DOV emphasis, and how the process of review and revisioning of this emphasis can best continue at the ninth assembly.

- A theme in missiology that emerged was that of the use, abuse and misuse of power, and how this relates to churches and agencies engaged in Christian mission.

- Agreement on the understanding of Christian witness in a religiously plural world is not easily achieved amid the expanded participation evident at this meeting; on the whole, the common approach to inter-religious dia-

Left: An Afghan child flies a kite at the Shamshatoo refugee camp near Peshawar, Pakistan. Kite flying was prohibited in Afghanistan under the Taliban government. Right: Members of the African Church of the Holy Spirit prepare to march in procession to Sunday morning worship in Kenya.

63

logue holds firm to the dual principles of the 1989 San Antonio mission conference, recognizing that, although we cannot place limits on God's grace, we also realize that we have been called as Christians to proclaim Jesus as Lord and Saviour.

- The "great new fact of our time" in mission today is to be found in the phenomenon that the *International Review of Mission* has called "the southern trajectory" of Christianity; the demographic centre of the faith continues to migrate from North to South, with the result that more and more mission carries the gospel message and its implications from South to North.

Next steps in mission

During the "sending service" at the Areopagus on the final evening of the Athens mission conference, Samuel Kobia gave this interpretation of the events of Pentecost: "The gospel is not our gospel that is to be translated from our language and experience to others for their benefit; rather, the gospel is that good news of Jesus Christ that all are privileged to hear, and the unity of what we hear overcomes the diversity of who we are. As Christians, we are members of a fellowship that exceeds our capacity to define it."

Even as studies, agreements, training and world conferences help point more churches towards the need for mission in unity, the task seems limitless. One of the strengths of the ecumenical movement's work in mission has been that it is approached from many different perspectives. Expanding participation in this essential dimension of the churches' task offers encouragement to those surveying the fields ripe for harvest. The labourers, however few, are increasing in numbers and enthusiasm, and are preparing to cooperate more closely. As they prayed at Athens, "Come, Holy Spirit!"

The activities described in this chapter are the primary responsibility of the Mission and Ecumenical Formation staff team.

The neighbourhood of El Cantaro in Tebaida, Colombia, was devastated by the January 1999 earthquake. Assistance came through the ACT network and especially the Mennonite Development Foundation of Colombia.

Churches respond to HIV and AIDS

When the assembly, and subsequent meetings of the central committee, addressed the need to combat HIV and AIDS, particularly in Africa, they were responding to obvious and tragic facts.

In its 2004 report on the global AIDS epidemic, UNAIDS estimated that 38 million adults and children were living with HIV around the globe. Twenty-five million are in sub-Saharan Africa. In 2003, an estimated 4.8 million people became newly infected with HIV, more than in any one year before. Almost 3 million people with AIDS died in 2003, and over 20 million since the first cases of AIDS in 1981.

Virtually no country is unaffected, and some countries that have "let down their guard" in prevention efforts witnessed a rise in the numbers of people infected with HIV.

Eastern Europe and East Asia are now experiencing the fastest-growing HIV epidemic in the world. Women and children are increasingly vulnerable.

The response of churches and other faith-based communities is widespread, but until recently largely undocumented. The WCC, which itself has worked on HIV/AIDS since the 1980s, published a report on "Responses of the Faith-Based Organizations to HIV/AIDS in Sub-Saharan Africa" which noted that "congregations and parishes have themselves been in the forefront of care and support right across Africa. A great number of these initiatives did not wait for funding in order to begin, they just responded."

As the WCC report also noted, faith-based organizations have also been

Peter Piot speaks at an ecumenical gathering on "Access for All: The Faith Community Responding", Bangkok, July 2004.

"It is time that UNAIDS and other UN agencies further recognized the tremendous potential of churches and faith-based organizations and involved them in the planning, implementation and monitoring of HIV/AIDS programmes at local, national and international level. In the WCC, we recognize that church leadership needs to mobilize communities to equip them not only to take care of the sick and suffering, but also to prevent the spread of HIV/AIDS."

Manoj Kurian, *WCC staff executive for health and healing, before the Special Session of the UN general assembly on HIV/AIDS, New York, June 2001*

65

"I hope for a day when every church engages in an open dialogue on issues of sexuality and gender difference. I hope for a day when every synagogue will mobilize as advocates for a global response to fight AIDS, when every temple will fully welcome people living with HIV, when every mosque is a place where young people will learn about the facts of HIV and AIDS. When that will have happened, I am convinced that nothing will stop our success in our fight against AIDS."

Dr Peter Piot, *executive director of UNAIDS, at an ecumenical pre-conference to the International AIDS Conference, July 2004*

"It is now common knowledge that in HIV/AIDS it is not the condition itself that hurts most (because many other diseases and conditions lead to serious suffering and death), but the stigma and the possibility of rejection and discrimination, misunderstanding and loss of trust that HIV positive people have to deal with."

Rev. Gideon Byamugisha, *global consultation on ecumenical response to HIV/AIDS in Africa, Nairobi, November 2001*

accused of silence, discrimination, stigmatization and harsh moral pronouncements which have obstructed efforts at care and prevention.

Thus WCC efforts have been on many levels: encouraging international recognition and support of faith-based efforts in the treatment and care of people living with HIV or AIDS, strengthening the faith-based response through training, information-sharing and networking; and, perhaps most importantly, working

to eradicate the silence, denial, stigma and discrimination within the church which has made so many spiritually homeless and prevented them from getting life-saving, accurate information and treatment.

The WCC carried out a mapping exercise in 29 African countries to gather vital information on the churches' response to HIV and AIDS. Consultations to share responses from Africa and Asia encouraged people in different regions to learn from the African experience.

The WCC is active in the HIV and AIDS campaign of the Ecumenical Advocacy Alliance, seeking to eradi-

Above: The Rev. Canon Gideon Byamugisha of Uganda, founder of the African Network of Religious Leaders Living with or Affected by HIV or AIDS. Below: A billboard in Port-au-Prince, Haiti, commends the use of condoms to fight HIV/AIDS.

66

cate stigma and discrimination associated with HIV and AIDS, advocate for adequate access to drugs and treatment, and raise awareness among church-related organizations and communities about basic facts of the disease and need for prevention.

The WCC enables faith-based participation at major UN meetings, such as the special session of the UN general assembly on HIV/AIDS in June 2001, to apply pressure on governments and intergovernmental organizations to provide the necessary resources and political will to tackle the pandemic. The WCC facilitates delegations at major conferences, such as the international AIDS conferences held every two years, the most recent in Bangkok in 2004.

The WCC hosted key regional consultations among the churches, particularly in Africa and Eastern Europe, to help develop plans of action with local, national and regional partners. One result of this work is the Ecumenical HIV/AIDS Initiative in Africa.

Ecumenical HIV/AIDS Initiative in Africa

In November 2001, at a global consultation on ecumenical responses to the challenges of HIV/AIDS in Africa, African and international church leaders and ecumenical organizations developed a coordinated plan of action, enabled by a support structure under the WCC. The Ecumenical HIV/AIDS Initiative in Africa (EHAIA) was launched in February 2002.

"Religious leaders are in a unique position to influence and inspire. They can reach into people's hearts and minds in a way no other group can. They can change norms and values. In many countries, faith-based committees and societies are also the best civil-society network in existence. Religious leaders must realize the power they have in the fight against HIV/AIDS, and use it to the fullest."

Hilde Johnson, *Norway's minister of international development, at a satellite session of the International AIDS Conference in Bangkok, July 2004*

67

Baker Sekiziyrvu of Buwama, Uganda (centre) was 13 when his parents died of AIDS, four years before this photo was taken, leaving him to care for younger brothers and sisters Andrew Kakumirizi (12 years old in the photo), Marry Nakyeyune (13), Annet Nakambala (16) and Paul Senyanga (11).

The EHAIA works to enable churches and ecumenical partners to have a full understanding of the severity of the HIV/AIDS epidemic in Africa and to reach out and respond in collaborative efforts to address the challenges it poses. Facilitated by four regional coordinators in each sub-region of Africa, along with a consultant for HIV/AIDS in theological training and mission, the programme is overseen by a project manager based at the WCC in Geneva.

The EHAIA developed education resources and networks on HIV/AIDS for church leaders, clergy and multipliers in church contexts and focused on building the capacity of churches and related organizations in the area of prevention, care and counselling. It provided practical support for congregations dealing with HIV/AIDS, including assistance to highly vulnerable groups such as orphans and prisoners, as well as infected clergy. It also strengthened church-related health care and pastoral counselling initiatives.

Billboard for condom use in Kampala, Uganda, April 2004.

Strong emphasis has been placed on gender issues and relations in families, churches and related institutions where changes in attitudes and situations are needed to remedy the particular vulnerability of women and girls to infection.

Dozens of workshops and other events were organized by the EHAIA staff throughout Africa with the churches and always involving people living with HIV/AIDS. Training-of-trainers workshops focused on teachers of religion and theology. Meetings of church leaders and NGOs were held in several sub-regions and national training events were held in several countries with the councils of churches. Focus groups for training included women's groups, pastors and other clergy, and youth – all have a multiplying role in prevention and education.

To raise awareness and support prevention and education, a number of books and other materials in English and French were published, including *AfricaPraying: A Handbook on HIV/AIDS Sensitive Sermon Guidelines and Liturgy; Modèles de prédication et de méditation biblique dans le contexte de VIH/SIDA en Afrique; HIV/AIDS and the Curriculum: Methods of Integrating HIV/AIDS in Theological Programmes,* and *Responses of the Faith-Based Organizations to HIV/AIDS in Sub-Saharan Africa.* A newsletter, a website (www.wcc-coe.org/wcc/what/mission/ehaia-e.html), and a CD-ROM with all WCC HIV/AIDS related resources in various languages also help share information and provide a platform for exchange.

Given the scope of the pandemic, churches are repeatedly invited to use their special access to the people and continue to learn, to speak and to act, in order to adjust their ministry to the threatening and overwhelming tasks set out before them in times of HIV.

69

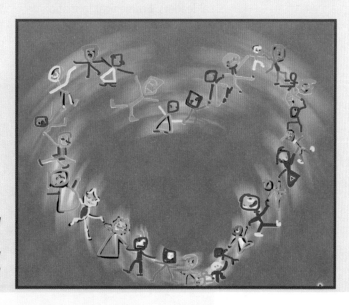

Seal of the Ecumenical HIV/AIDS Initiative in Africa, set up as a joint undertaking of churches and agencies from south and north in 2002.

Education as Ecumenical Formation

Education in a variety of guises helps to form new participants and leaders in the ecumenical movement; the process of "formation" shapes and equips us for opportunities in ministry. New initiatives in ecumenical formation and resources have been developed in the years since the Harare assembly. The willingness to tackle cutting-edge issues gives vibrancy to the Ecumenical Institute of Bossey as an ecumenical learning "laboratory". Supporting scholars around the world, ecumenical academies and networks, and exploring the new territory of interfaith religious education are the vital foundations for the ecumenical movement today and in the future.

Memory, energy and vision sustain movements into the future. Any movement, then, must renew, inspire and recommit people to its principles and mission. The ecumenical movement faces this challenge by seeking new ways to renew ecumenical consciousness in a divided world and build a new generation of ecumenical leaders. Ecumenical formation itself is a process of theological reflection and critical thinking that moves beyond learning about one another within the church to learning from and with one another. The WCC seeks to create spaces where people learn in community, and where they encounter different cultures and traditions.

Renewing ecumenical spirit in the regions

The Ecumenical Theological Education (ETE) programme pro-

Speakers at the children's padare at the eighth assembly in Harare, December 1998.

motes ecumenical theological education and ministerial formation for the renewal and unity of the church. By supporting local projects, forming and enabling regional networks and associations, and promoting theological educators and students, new and creative methods for ecumenical theological education are explored.

Efforts since Harare have concentrated on Central and Eastern Europe, Asia and Pacific, Latin America and Africa. Consultants to assist the programme were named in the past several years in three regions: in the Asia/Pacific region in collaboration with the Christian Conference of Asia, in Latin America/Caribbean in cooperation with a biblical university based in Costa Rica, and in Central and Eastern Europe with a special concern for Orthodox theological education.

In Central and Eastern Europe, the WCC has accompanied the member churches and theological institutions in addressing theological or religious education after the fall of communism. The regional consultant, based in St Petersburg, Russia, works full-time to raise awareness of the need for ecumenical theological education and develop networks.

In 2003, a consultation on "Ecumenical Cooperation on Theological and Religious Education in Post-Communist Europe" was held. Through this consultation, participants from different theological institutions in post-communist countries met for the first time to discuss with their Western colleagues the challenges of the new Europe and ways of renewing theological education with an ecumenical perspective. The ideas and recommendations from the consultation continue to form the basis for building exchanges and networks.

Theological education that addresses HIV/AIDS has been particularly critical in Africa. The ETE worked closely with the theological consultant for the Ecumenical HIV/AIDS Initiative in Africa (p. 67) to develop curriculum and approach theological institutions with proposals for training of trainers workshops.

Wahone Mutake, author of the play "A Journey of Hope", with WCC deputy general secretary Mercy Oduyoye at the Africa plenary of the Harare assembly, December 1998.

About 7000 people, mostly Dalits and Indigenous people, live in Arjun camp at the end of the main runway of New Delhi's international airport.

Empowerment of women in theological education has taken place particularly in Francophone Africa and Kenya and through supporting the Circle of Concerned African Women Theologians in creating a theological curriculum on gender and theology. The "Journey of Hope" consultation (see Focus on Africa p. 144) resulted in the development of African pastoral theology and ethics and a theological curriculum on violence against children and women, especially in conflict areas.

In Asia and the Pacific, attention was given in particular to Cambodia and Vietnam through several visits and support to encourage the churches, struggling against many odds, as they restructure ecumenical theological education through Bible schools and theological education by extension programmes.

A regional forum for associations of theological librarians was revitalized to enable training programmes, resource-sharing, networking and publication.

Workshops for theological teachers were held in South Asia, focusing on overcoming violence and HIV and AIDS. A workshop on equipping women for transformational leadership in 2003 brought together fifty women theological administrators and educators from south-east Asia, India and Sri Lanka in a cooperative effort with several regional and national associations.

Several key visits of ETE staff and theological educators to China have led to a rich exchange of resources and learning. Other workshops for educators are held on a national or sub-regional basis.

In the Pacific, links have been made with the Pacific Theological College and the theological association and a discussion forum created to connect theological associations in Asia and the Pacific to increase ecumenical consciousness in the two regions.

In Latin America and the Caribbean, a workshop on ecumenism held in 2003 in Costa Rica brought together 45 leaders of Christian base communities from 14 countries in the region. Training of Indigenous pastors and theological educators, and the formation of an association, will facilitate new, creative ecumenical programmes for Indigenous pastors.

Overall, the regional consultants screen applications for grants for faculty development and library development, which are decided by the ETE working group. The working group meets annually to reflect on and analyze regional theological education trends and opportunities from an ecumenical perspective.

Because of the needs in these regions and lack of funds to expand, networking and relationships in the Middle East, Western Europe and North America have not been able to progress as hoped, but connections through speaking engagements and resource-sharing are still made.

Supporting ecumenical education and responding to new challenges

WCC staff meet with theological educators around the world to network, share resources and learn more about needs and trends. Consultations with educators are held regionally to discuss themes together. Regional associations of

Theological students at the Christian university in Tomohon, North Sulawesi, Indonesia.

Education only in and about one's own tradition deprives people of the richness and diversity of the human community. Knowledge and experience of the religious lives of those among whom we live help us to have a feel of what it means to be part of the wider human community.

From an open letter by educators from Buddhist, Christian, Jewish, Muslim, Sikh and Indigenous Filipino traditions*, October 2000*

74

theological education institutions often include churches outside WCC membership, such as Pentecostal and African-Instituted churches. Staff engage with ecumenical educational networks to encourage good ecumenical and learning practices. They support faculty development, especially of women, library and literature development, and strengthen the self-reliance of advanced theological education systems in the South.

Advocacy for women in theological education is important in WCC work. During the Ecumenical Decade of the Churches in Solidarity with Women, the International Feminist Doctoral of Ministry Programme was established in which over eighty women have enrolled and from which 15 have graduated. A global campaign to

fund the Sarah Chakko Theological Endowment Fund to support women's ecumenical education has also begun.

The WCC organizes annually a meeting of the ecumenical officers of churches – a group of about eighty church staff – for networking and information-sharing. A growing need to support women ecumenical officers and to better equip women to serve in that capacity was identified and several training and reflection seminars were held beginning in June 2001.

Knowledge of ecumenical history and principles cannot be assumed even for WCC and other ecumenical staff. New learning resources and opportunities for ecumenical learning

Students in a rural school in Jaldhaka district, Dinajpur province, Bangladesh.

have been created for the staff of the WCC and its partners.

The WCC is making more of its educational resources available on-line and encourages public discussion and interaction. Short and simple "Good Practice Guides for Ecumenical Learning" are available through *www.ecuspace.net* along with research results into ecumenical learning.

A bi-annual publication, *EEF-NET*, serves educators within the churches and ecumenical bodies. Produced in English, Spanish and French, it is available in print as well as on-line. The quarterly journal *Ministerial Formation* has been an effective instrument for keeping in touch with theological institutions and associations.

A WCC consultation of religious educators from six major world faiths was held in October 2000 in Bangkok and led to a challenge to faith communities and state schools systems to provide religious education that offers a sympathetic rather than a biased understanding of all faiths. In an open letter to religious educators around the world, the participants pointed out that learning about the faith of others not only helps eliminate violence and promote communal harmony but also can be a means of spiritual development within the learner's own religious tradition. The participants emphasized the need to affirm positive common ground between religions.

Interfaith learning has become one of the next large challenges of ecu-

A roadblock to normal life: children in Al-Izariyyeh (Bethany), Palestine, find their way blocked.

menical learning, and the WCC is working with NGOs and faith-based groups, as well as theological institutions which include interfaith education, to chart needs and ways forward.

The WCC has helped coordinate OIKOSNET – the global ecumenical network of Christian laity centres, academies and movements for social concern. The network links over six hundred Christian lay centres, academies and social movements which belong to seven regional associations.

OIKOSNET organizes one-month courses for lay leadership training (CLLTs) to train people for involvement in the ecumenical movement. A global CLLT planned for the Middle

East in late 2001 was postponed due to the world situation and was reorganized for June 2002. Under the theme "To be Instruments for Peace", the twenty international participants were sent in small groups to visit communities in Lebanon, Syria and Egypt, and they then followed a two-week residential course in Cyprus. The programme was jointly hosted by the Middle East Council of Churches and the Middle East Association of Training and Retreat Centres.

A Bulgarian Orthodox film producer was supported by the WCC under the resident journalist programme to accompany the CLLT. The resulting video, *Breaking Barriers*, documents the personal learning and transfor-

Community educators portray the suffering of Dalits in the form of a drama in Kanlvakam, 45 km south of Chennai/Madras, India.

mation that can take place through such ecumenical and multicultural encounters.

In 2003, the WCC turned over the coordination of the network and organization of the CLLTs to OIKOS-NET itself. The WCC continues to participate in OIKOSNET meetings and helps disseminate the learnings and experiences of the network through EEF-NET and the web.

The WCC Commission on Education and Ecumenical Formation is the primary point of assessment and reflection, meeting approximately every 18 months.

Scholarships

The scholarships programme, which has existed since 1945, provides resources and opportunities for individuals and groups to receive the training and ecumenical formation they need to serve their community better. Scholarships are offered to men and women, lay and ordained, usually under the age of 45, whose further education is important for future service to the church. Particular concern has been given to equal opportunities for women.

Respecting regional diversity and tailoring responses to meet regional needs, the programme supports a wide variety of training. In fact, currently the majority of awards are in non-theological study, helping to build capacity in areas such as community development, agronomy, law, education and health.

A network of national correspondents and committees gives priority to applications according to local need. The WCC scholarships committee seeks to ensure a fair distribution of funds available at a global level.

Along with offering scholarships to individuals for graduate study, the programme now supports group training, which has become a successful way to expand the benefit of learning throughout the community.

From 1999 to 2004, 463 individual scholarships and over 51 group scholarships were awarded. From 2004 to 2006, four thematic areas were given priority for study and training: interfaith relations, globalization, overcoming violence and HIV/AIDS.

The programme has developed many creative partnerships with theological seminaries and learning institutions throughout the world which support scholars and provide training and cultural exchange.

The activities described in this chapter are the primary responsibility of the Mission and Ecumenical Formation staff team.

77

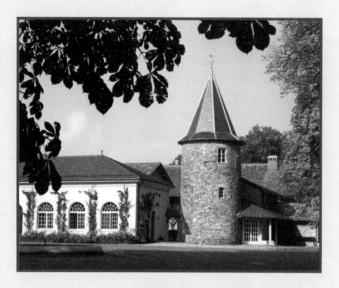

The Ecumenical Institute at Bossey, Switzerland, approximately 20 kilometres northeast of downtown Geneva.

The Ecumenical Institute at Bossey

The Harare assembly encouraged Bossey to strengthen links to its alumni, expand programmes for laity, build bridges with other institutes and explore creative ways of offering its rich resources at locations around the world. The period since Harare has seen a vast expansion of the Institute's potential. Indeed, Bossey represents one of the real success stories of the WCC during the period from Harare to Porto Alegre.

During these years Bossey undertook an extensive and highly successful renovation project to improve its accommodation, meeting facilities and library; but, more significantly, it has experienced a major renovation of its academic programme through strengthening the annual Graduate School of the Ecumenical Institute, adding masters degree and PhD programmes, and expanding its seminar offerings to include a month-long

session of interfaith encounter. These advances to both facilities and programme have not only stabilized the financial situation of Bossey, but also offered to the WCC growing partnerships with churches, international non-governmental agencies in Geneva, ecumenical and theological institutes and lay-training centres around the world.

Bossey's mission is to educate and form leaders, both clergy and lay, for service to the ecumenical movement in its local, regional and global expressions. It is often said that Bossey serves as a unique "laboratory for ecumenical education and formation" as it provides a free and safe space of mutual encounter and challenge for Christians all over the world.

The Ecumenical Institute plays a major role on behalf of the World Council of Churches in shaping ecumenical thought through intercultural and interconfessional encounter within the framework of worship, study, and life in community. Bossey offers programmes to address the most acute and contemporary challenges confronting the church in our world today. It has served as a place where, through study and research, life and encounter, people come to better understanding and appreciate their own traditions and identities within the context of the whole church.

In 2003 Bossey celebrated the fiftieth anniversary of the first graduate school along with the completion of the renovations of its facilities. The celebrations brought together alumni, friends, academic partners and members of the local community.

Fifty-seven sessions of the graduate school will have been held by the ninth assembly. In addition to core courses, the school follows a theme coming out of the experience of the ecumenical movement. The 57th session explored "grace, healing and transformation" – linking the themes of the ninth assembly and the world mission conference. Those who successfully complete the graduate school of ecumenical studies programme are granted a certificate of ecumenical studies from the Ecumenical Institute of Bossey.

A Master of ecumenical studies degree programme became a new addition to the curriculum, allowing a selected number of students to pursue study in a range of ecumenical subjects. A Ph.D. in ecumenics was begun in 2004. The Institute's academic courses are offered through a partnership with the autonomous faculty of Protestant theology of the University of Geneva.

To equip students with skills to assist them in international ecumenical work, intensive summer English-language courses are also offered now.

An annual seminar on Orthodox spirituality allows participants to deepen their understanding of the theology and prayer life of the Christian East.

Post-graduate school, spring 2003, at the Ecumenical Institute, Bossey.

Short-term seminars continue to be offered at Bossey on acute contemporary issues that confront and challenge churches. Topics have included religion and violence, Orthodox spirituality, science and faith, genetic engineering and human sexuality.

A programme was begun to enable those with expertise in the ecumenical field to teach up to one academic year as visiting professors, either on sabbatical leave or during retirement. The first visiting professor under the programme served in the 2004-2005 academic year through support by the friends of Bossey in the Netherlands.

A Bossey board, appointed by the WCC central committee, serves as an advisory group. A Bossey liaison group links WCC and Bossey staff in planning research and study options.

A major grant to the WCC for an ecumenical research centre from the Banque Pictet in Geneva allowed for the rebuilding of a larger and better equipped library facility at Bossey, the merger of the WCC and Bossey library, and new facilities and support for the ecumenical archives housed at the WCC in Geneva. The goal of this project has been to create the world's leading ecumenical research library (see Communicating the Ecumenical Story, p. 158).

The late Professor Faitala Talapusi of the Bossey faculty (standing) directs a "Pacific night" presentation during the 56th annual graduate school at the Ecumenical Institute, February 2005.

Engaging in Dialogue with Neighbours of Other Religions

When the WCC began work on inter-religious dialogue in 1971, few envisioned that inter-religious relationships and dialogue would be so critical in developing common responses to the violence, human-rights abuses, political tensions and religious intolerance now facing the local and global community. But by the central committee meeting in 2003, Catholicos Aram I, in his report as moderator, called for "dialogue, relations and collaboration with other religions" to be designated a "high priority" in the WCC's ecumenical witness.

The Harare assembly's programme guidelines committee noted repeatedly the importance of integrating inter-religious dialogue and relationships in the activities of the Council, particularly giving more attention to the religious dimensions of conflict. In its facilitation of dialogue between religions, the WCC encourages participants to reflect seriously on the relationship of religion to violence. Growing awareness of the reality of religious pluralism also led the committee to state that the WCC should have a "primary focus" in helping churches deal with "the theological, missiological and political challenges" of living in pluralistic societies.

Participants in inter-religious dialogue during the eighth assembly, Harare, December 1998.

The need for religious leaders and their constituencies to promote cooperation among diverse communities of faith has never been greater. Yet a religious organization such as the World Council of Churches must also counsel its constituency to embrace initiatives that seem most likely to contribute to the peace and greater justice sought by all. Such counsel is especially relevant for the WCC, as many now consider what "ecumenism" should mean as churches face greater religious pluralism.

WCC consultation on participation in multi-faith initiatives
HongKong, 2002

82

Discerning the WCC's role

The process of globalization combined with the "millennium syndrome" led to a proliferation of international multifaith initiatives hosted by the United Nations, international financial institutions, national governments and corporations. The WCC's long history in inter-religious dialogue has built trust among many partners, in addition to experience and expertise. Thus, the WCC has been repeatedly pressed to contribute leadership to many events.

WCC general secretary Konrad Raiser was invited to speak at one of the most ambitious of such events, the Millennium World Peace Summit of Religious and Spiritual Leaders, held in 2000. The summit was the first time religious and spiritual leaders came together on the invitation of UN secretary general Kofi Annan. The

event was important, Raiser underlined, for reflecting on the contribution of religious communities towards building a sustainable, just and peaceful world community. However, not least because of unbalanced representation, the conference had few concrete results.

The demands to participate in a variety of inter-religious initiatives prompted the consideration of how best the WCC could contribute its experience and expertise. A multifaith consultation in Hong Kong in April 2002 developed criteria to try to express the wide variety of purposes involved in carrying out multifaith work, discuss collaboration with international inter-religious organizations, reflect on questions related to the possibilities for a common religious agenda, and address the establishment of inter-religious councils.

A Taoist prayer gathering at the multifaith consultation on international inter-religious initiatives, Tao Fong Shan, Hong Kong, April 2002.

Christian-Muslim dialogue

For many, September 11, 2001 changed global priorities for inter-religious cooperation. The attacks on the World Trade Center and the Pentagon by extremists who evoked faith language awoke many to the reality of religious plurality locally, nationally and internationally – and made people acutely aware of how little communities know and understand the beliefs and practices in their midst. Suspicion, fear and even hostility across religious boundaries were exacerbated.

The executive committee, meeting in Geneva at the same time as the attacks, immediately encouraged a wide distribution of a new WCC publication, even more relevant in the global crisis, *Striving Together for Dialogue: A Christian-Muslim Call to Reflection and Action.*

Striving Together for Dialogue was developed by Christians and Muslims, through the years 1998-2000, out of the WCC's three decades of Christian-Muslim dialogue, and draws on reflections over the previous nine years by Christian and Muslim religious leaders, educators and activists who have been engaged in discussing the thorny and sometimes divisive issues of religion, law and society, human rights, religious freedom, community rights, mission and *da'wa* and communal tensions. In many parts of the world, Christian-Muslim dialogue was intensified or accelerated after September 11. The WCC played a leading role in initiating or accompanying Christian-Muslim discussions that did not shy away from addressing conflictive attitudes and looking into the religious and political roots of both misunderstanding and divergence.

Left: Marcelo Barros, a Benedictine monk, and Querina dos Santos, a theologian of the Candomblé religion, meet at the World Social Forum, Porto Alegre, January 2003. Right: Believers from eight different religions join n a prayer for peace at the World Social Forum in Porto Alegre.

83

The Orthodox church in Kejveo, Kosovo, near Prishtina, was blown up in the conflict there.

Immediately following September 11, the WCC continued with renewed commitment intensive contacts already initiated with its Muslim partners to respond to the critical political situation that marked relations between, and within, nations, and its impact on Christian-Muslim relationships – at the international level, in the Middle East and elsewhere in countries with a Muslim majority. The WCC joined with a number of partners, including the Vatican's Pontifical Council for Inter-religious Dialogue and with Muslim leaders, for a series of consultations later in 2001 promoting dialogue for the sake of understanding and peace.

These consultations were held in Cairo in October and December 2001 and were facilitated by the WCC with the Middle East Council of Churches. They looked at the situation locally, regionally and internationally to assess the impact of September 11 and the resulting "war on terrorism". The final seminar with 45 scholars and leaders engaged in Christian-Muslim dialogue from the Arab world, the USA, Europe and Asia proposed that the mutual interpretation of each others' religion, the discussion of the history of violence, the notions of Jihad and "just war", as well as the impact of global religious confrontation on local relations should be among the main areas on which Christian-Muslim dialogue should focus in the future.

While Muslim leaders attempted to gain visibility for the message that acts of terrorism in the name of Islam pervert the faith, Christian leaders, particularly the WCC, worked to counter the perception, particularly in the Muslim world, that the resulting "war on terrorism" in the way and scope in which it was unleashed, including the attacks on

Afghanistan and Iraq, were condoned by the Christian faith.

In November 2001, Konrad Raiser sent a letter to the heads of Muslim religious communities throughout the world at the beginning of the Muslim month of fasting in Ramadan which coincided with the Christian Advent. He called for genuine cooperation and joint efforts to assist victims, to defend human rights and humanitarian law and for "intensification of dialogue between religions and cultures". The letter was warmly received by Muslim leaders and communities and opened new partnerships that helped to pave the way for deeper dialogue.

The WCC's efforts led to a high-level consultation on "Christians and Muslims in Dialogue and Beyond" in October 2002, which looked at the present state of Christian-Muslim relations where difficulties experi-

enced need not overshadow the friendly and neighbourly relations that people have built through the years and deepened through dialogue and cooperation. The conference also emphasized the conditions for a real change to happen in the broader communities where Christians and Muslims live and work together. Issues of human rights and citizenship and those of seeking justice and overcoming violence were debated in great openness.

In 2003, Christians and Muslims meeting in London reflected on the way political tensions and conflicts, mostly involving the Arab world and the USA, were impacting relations between Muslims and Christians throughout the world. The meeting offered thoughts on the controversies over values, religious or secular, that are said to exacerbate divisions between the "Western world" and the "Muslim world". In the same

A Palestinian Christian in the West Bank village of Aboud, a member of the Greek Orthodox church there, holds a cross that he has carved.

In a context where religions are finding renewed public vigour, issues of freedom of conscience and human rights generally have re-emerged, in the last few years, as sensitive and even divisive. In this respect, Christian-Muslim dialogue has an indispensable contribution to make in affirming that the principles of human rights and religious freedom are indivisible. It is called to direct the forces of religiosity towards common good, instead of allowing them to breed intra-religious and inter-religious hatred and conflicts.

Striving Together for Dialogue

86

vein, Christian-Muslim meetings were held in Iran and Turkey.

The visit of the Iranian President Muhammad Khatami to the WCC in December 2003 was yet another powerful sign that Christian-Muslim dialogue, at every level, is urgent and needs to be broadened both in terms of partners and issues.

Religion and violence

While work on religion and violence intensified after 2001, the WCC had long been dealing with the issue. The central committee was also clear from the beginning of the Decade to Overcome Violence that people of other faiths were important partners, and interfaith efforts to build a culture of non-violence should be sought actively.

The WCC, in different forums, addressed the situation of Christian minorities, particularly those caught

in the midst of conflicts with religious overtones. It continued to promote actively inter-religious cooperation and dialogue in conflict situations, particularly in the Former Yugoslav Republic of Macedonia, Sierra Leone and Indonesia, and monitored and addressed issues of religious freedom and religious intolerance in a number of countries as a human-rights issue.

Youth became important partners in addressing religion and violence, not only to help them cope in their own contexts but to enable them to become leaders in their communities in peace-building efforts. In 2001, a meeting in Indonesia brought together youth from several countries experiencing conflict related to religion. In the meeting, youth from both sides of each conflict developed a joint three-year action plan to help build peace in their community.

The cross on the Greek Orthodox church in Zababdeh, Occupied Palestinian Territories, stands near the neighbouring minaret of a mosque.

Another inter-religious youth workshop held in the Middle East in 2004 brought together young Christians and Muslims from the region to build a common vision of peace and non-violent action. This workshop encouraged participants to discuss educational alternatives towards a culture of non-violence and provide training in dialogue and reconciliation.

The theological and cultural questions regarding religion and violence were directly addressed beginning in 2002 through the WCC and the Bossey Ecumenical Institute's annual Visser 't Hooft memorial consultations. The inter-religious dialogue on religion and violence continued over three seminars which brought participants from Christian, Muslim, Jewish, Hindu, Buddhist and Indigenous traditions together to explore the relationship between religion, power and violence. In a result-ing video, *Religion, Power and Violence*, participants ponder the issues around religion and violence, and ask what it really means to be truly human and to recognize the other – even on the adversaries' side – as truly human. The video is accompanied by a study guide for use by various communities living in multicultural contexts.

The question of religion and violence was also addressed in a multifaith seminar in St Petersburg, Florida, USA, in 2002 which emphasized a self-critical examination of the interaction of religion and violence. The seminar acknowledged that each religion upholds an ideal of peace, yet the inescapable reality is that religious justification is often used for violence,

"The enfolding realities and crises of the world urge all religions to move from mere reaction to common response. 'Being ecumenical' is a challenge to all religions. Dialogue is the only way for religions to become pro-active, the only way for them to articulate their common voice concretely and to participate actively in the transformation of society."

Report of His Holiness Aram I, *moderator of the central committee 2003*

87

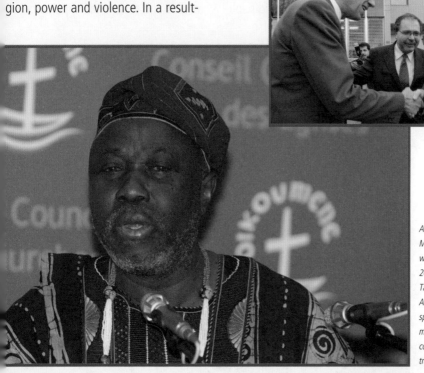

Above: Iranian president Mohammed Khatani is welcomed to the WCC in 2003 by Konrad Raiser and Tarek Mitri. Left: Dr Wande Abimbola of Nigeria speaks to the "critical moment" conference on African traditional Religions.

that religious tradition is found on the side of the powerful who oppress the powerless, that religion cannot be considered "an innocent bystander" in conflict. The assessment of reality, the seminar stressed, as opposed to ideal, is the first step in seriously addressing the role of religions in violence.

Common responses to critical issues

In 2001, the central committee echoed the Harare assembly's concern that the WCC increasingly explore with partners of other faith communities how common commitments to human rights and dignity can be translated into a global framework of values to which all can subscribe.

Directly in response to the assembly concern regarding the theological, political and missiological challenges of religious plurality, a multidiscipli-

nary and multifaith study involving the networks of Faith and Order, the Commission on World Mission and Evangelism and the Office on Inter-religious Relations and Dialogue began in 2003 to provide a theologically comprehensive view of Christian identity in a religiously pluralistic world. A study document was produced entitled "Religious Plurality and Christian Self-Understanding".

Inter-religious dialogue "critical moment" conference

More than a hundred people from most of the world's religious traditions met together at the "critical moment in inter-religious dialogue" conference which was held in Geneva, 7-9 June 2005, convened by the WCC.

The conference aimed to analyze, assess and review the experience of

inter-religious collaboration and dialogue as it has been practised over recent decades and might be undertaken in the future. During the event, religious scholars, academics, human-rights activists, humanitarian workers, journalists and other people experienced in working across religious traditions discussed the themes of "thinking together", "assessing the present" and "imagining the future".

"Recasting inter-religious dialogue as a practice of humility and hope offers a way of building greater trust," concluded participants in the international conference. "Together, may we seize this critical moment and help transform its perils into a pilgrimage of faith that will guide us to a more just, compassionate and peaceful future." The conference was an opportunity to address inter-religious tensions and divides, the present state of relations between religious communities, and the challenges facing people in today's world. It sought to provide a forum for bridge-building conversations that focus on social-justice issues despite religious differences.

The conference outlined specific strategies which aim to shift the emphasis of inter-religious relations from dialogue to common action, including new education and training programmes and exchanges that foster a culture of dialogue. Symbolic actions promoting healing of historical memory, new structures, networks and action plans at the national and regional levels were upheld as practical examples to be followed up. The meeting also enabled open discussion of divisive issues, notably those of religious violence and conversion, and called for repentance and humility that

Opposite: A Muslim man and his prayer beads in the West Bank village of Aboud.

Below: Plenary session at the "critical moment" inter-religious conference of 2005: Dr Oddbjørn Leirvik, Norway, Dr Brijinder Singh Rattah, India, and Dr Meehyun Chung, Switzerland.

89

"open a way to move from a dialogue of strangers to a dialogue of neighbours".

Referring to the conference as a "landmark event", the WCC leadership reiterated the strengthened commitment of the worldwide fellowship of Christian churches to interfaith dialogue and understanding. "Dialogue with other faiths has become a core issue for the WCC," confirmed WCC general secretary Samuel Kobia. "We can only be effective and successful in our search for hope if we work together. Together, we can go far towards restoring hope for another possible and better world in which all people may experience abundant life in dignity."

Guidance to churches

Fundamentally, the WCC's work on inter-religious dialogue is aimed at listening to churches' concerns, help-

ing member churches engage in dialogue in their own contexts, deal with religious plurality and seek ways to live, work and pray with their neighbours of other faiths.

The WCC revised its popular *Guidelines for Dialogue* for churches and ecumenical partners involved in inter-religious concerns. The text, reviewed by the central committee in 2002, was then published as *Ecumenical Considerations for Dialogue and Relations with People of Other Religions*, and made available in several languages. The WCC has received many requests from inter-religious partners to publish the document for their own communities.

Churches have been helped by the WCC in inter-religious issues not only through the published fruits of dialogue, but also through exchanges facilitated across countries and

Seyed Mohammed Ali Abtahi of Iran chats with Yehuda Stolov of Israel at the "critical moment in inter-religious dialogue" conference, Geneva 2005.

90

regions. Churches call on the WCC for advice, contacts and assistance in bilaterial and multilateral initiatives to address common issues and divisive questions. The diverse relations the WCC establishes and cultivates with various representative organizations of other faith traditions and inter-religious bodies have assisted the whole fellowship of churches better to understand the church's witness in the contemporary world.

New understandings

Multifaith meetings explore what can be achieved when people of different faiths do their thinking not just in awareness of each other's existence, but in each other's presence. These efforts can lead to new self-understandings, and better understandings as communities and institutions.

This objective is behind a joint WCC-International Council of Christians and Jews study, initiated in 2002, on the inter-relationship of Jewish-Christian dialogue and the churches' self-understanding.

Such motivation is also behind the multifaith process of thinking together where, since 1999, a group of clergy, educators and academics from the Buddhist, Christian, Hindu, Jewish and Muslim faiths have reflected together upon issues of concern in our religious traditions in a world of religious plurality. The meetings focused on the challenge of religious plurality, on religion and violence and under the title "from xenophobia to philoxenia" – from fear and hatred of foreigners to, literally, "the love of strangers" – on the role of "the Other" in our religious traditions. Specific approaches to engage local communities in inter-religious dialogue were developed by exploring past and present religious

Below left: Buddhist participants in the interfaith service of prayer and meditation during the XVth International AIDS Conference. Right: The old mosque of Sarajevo, Bosnia-Herzogovina.

91

Memory is foundational and is celebrated in a liturgical manner in the theology of reconstruction. Countries, cultures, dignity have been destroyed repeatedly and yet one has to assume the responsibility to deal with memory in a constructive way… There is a need to think in terms of reparation and not in terms of retribution – or else the whole population is imprisoned.

Reflections from the African French-speaking Christian-Jewish consultation,
November 2001

Left: In April 1994, thousands fled to the church at Ntarama, Rwanda, in search of sanctuary. Instead, they were shot or hacked to death. Right: Muslim participant Mahmoud Mohammadi Araghi of Iran follows the dialogue at the WCC-sponsored "critical moment" conference of June 2005.

definitions, texts and traditions. The group's goal is to provide inter-religious considerations for living in dialogue adapted for local congregations, bringing together material on themes discussed, such as "religious plurality", "religion and violence" and "the role and place of the Other in our religious tradition" into a multifaith publication.

The WCC has also opened up discussions with people of Indigenous beliefs and of African traditional spiritualities (see Focus on Africa, p. 144).

In its annual meeting with the WCC's inter-religious counterparts in the Vatican, the question of proselytism has also been discussed in the context of Hindu-Christian relations. In 2005 a preparatory reflection began, which is to involve a hearing with people of other faiths, theological work on the issue of conversion, and development of a common statement or code of conduct. The expected result of the Vatican-WCC project on conversion should provide a safe space for people of different faiths to voice their concerns and contribute to a common

understanding of religious liberty and respect for religious plurality.

The WCC continues to bring the issue of Jewish-Christian dialogue beyond North America and Western Europe. The question of religions and violence was addressed at the first-ever African, French-speaking, Christian-Jewish consultation, co-organized by the WCC and the International Jewish Committee for Inter-religious Relations, held in Yaoundé, Cameroon, in November 2001. Focused on the concepts of *shalom* and *ubuntu* and challenges in peace-making, the consultation also dealt with memories and experiences of violence. Special emphasis was put on responses to the Shoah (holocaust) and the genocide in Rwanda. The discussion between African Christians and Jews focused on concepts such as retributive justice, the reconstruction of community and reconciliation. A book, published simultaneously in Hebrew, French and English, entitled *Worlds of Memory and Wisdom: Encounters of Jews and African Christians*, provides an illustration

92

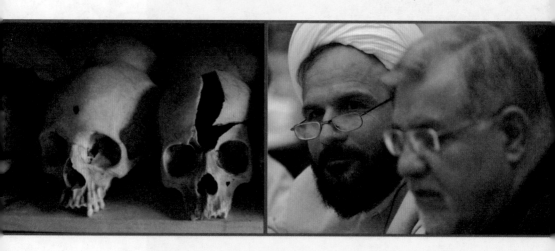

of the many affinities between the Jewish and African traditions.

The WCC, through a grant from Banque Pictet in Geneva for inter-religious work, is providing content for an inter-religious manifestation in Geneva in the autumn of 2005. One focus is on a multifaith manifesto encouraging young people to affirm plurality. Young people in Geneva will receive, study and relate to the document alongside high-profile religious and cultural personalities.

Current Dialogue is published twice a year and is available on the web and in hard copy as a steady source of the learnings and new opportunities for inter-religious dialogue. Contributors and readers include people of other faiths.

Through all these efforts, the WCC seeks to develop greater awareness in the ecumenical movement of the importance of inter-religious relations, and to promote the integration of inter-religious dialogue in the different ministries of the church, such as in youth work, education, peace and reconciliation, and social justice.

Above all, the WCC seeks greater awareness among churches, political and civil-society entities, and faith partners, that dialogue is not "an ambulance" that can suddenly be started in a time of crisis. Indeed, a crisis can be too late to start dialogue. Rather, dialogue is preventive

Below left: Mosque in Tirana, Albania; followers of Islam make up 70 percent of the national population. Right: The church of Michael and Gabriel in Goranxi, Albania.

93

– a steady and sometimes painfully slow process of building understanding and trust that helps to avoid or resolve crises.

Some have begun to apply an early ecumenical principle to inter-religious relationships: "That which we can do together, we should not do separately." Given the challenges of the contemporary world, this may be fundamental to overcoming violence and building just and sustainable communities.

The Pro Vita project cares for former street children from Bucharest in the Transylvanian mountain village of Valea Oltului, Romania.

The activities described in this chapter are the primary responsibility of the Inter-religious Relations and Dialogue staff team.

94

Serving Human Need

The WCC is a leading advocate for uprooted people – for their rights, for just and humane treatment, for emergency relief as well as for the resolution of the root causes which drive people from their homes. Such a comprehensive approach is part of diakonia – the service ministry of the church inspired by the calling of the first deacons in Acts 6 – where the WCC serves as a vital platform for churches and organizations to determine together their needs for support, mutual relationship, accountability and sustainability.

Calling the churches to unity beckons them to turn, in response to God's transforming love in Christ, to the world's suffering and need, and to act together.

Harare assembly programme guidelines committee

The WCC aims to strengthen ecumenical cooperation in the area of practical service, capacity-building and development cooperation worldwide. The WCC is a leader in international advocacy for uprooted people. Its sustained presence and support helps the international community respond effectively to crises.

The WCC creates platforms where such exchanges can take place, helps churches and ecumenical organizations build and strengthen their capacity to deal with the challenges facing their communities, and facilitates study and reflection on dia-

Caring for life calls for service (diakonia) to the world as essential to our life together as churches in Christ.

Central committee, 1999

95

Partnership and ecumenical priorities for diakonia

Over the past decades the ecumenical family has grown in its awareness that diakonia is far more than giving money, and instead involves the development of partnerships with churches, agencies and specialized ministries and shared planning and implementation. Diakonia recognizes that resources – material, financial, human and spiritual – flow among all the partners.

The medical needs of the people of the Solomon Islands are addressed by the Helena Goldie Hospital in Munda, New George Island.

their diaconal work and to develop consensus regarding ecumenical principles of cooperation and a fair distribution of funds in response to global ecumenical priorities. An increasingly competitive market for development funds places pressures on church-related organizations from their own funding bodies, and new demands in reporting and demonstrating "success" in order to continue to receive funds brought about a major shift from such multi-lateral sharing to primarily bilateral sharing – direct funding from one partner to another.

96

Volunteers in Tirana, Albania, deliver relief supplies to refugees from the fighting in Kosovo, April 1999.

konia and solidarity as an essential part of Christian witness.

How financial resources are used still remains one of the most visible aspects of diakonia. The period after Harare has seen a very significant shift in how project funds are channelled, particularly from churches and church-related agencies in the North to churches and community projects in the South.

In the past, the WCC channelled funds from the churches and agencies primarily in the North and distributed them to areas and projects according to the funder's guidelines. The WCC did not simply administer the funds, however, but sought to accompany and support churches in

While most of the funds now provided by the ecumenical family are channelled directly to partners, the WCC still coordinates mechanisms that assist all the partners – international, regional and national – to identify priorities and develop effective projects jointly. And the WCC seeks to keep before the entire ecumenical family larger global realities that must be addressed – and the resources needed to support them.

Ecumenical regional group meetings are held each year in the Pacific, Asia, Africa, Middle East, Latin America, the Caribbean and Europe as an opportunity for churches and ecumenical agencies to analyze the situation of churches and ecumenical life and to deepen theological reflection on diakonia and justice. The regional groups, which include the regional ecumenical organizations, help to set broad priorities for ecumenical work in the year ahead.

Round-table programmes, organized usually on a national basis, also bring national and international partners together to discuss priorities, projects and approach. The WCC facilitates over fifty round tables or equivalent forums around the world. Round tables have proved very effective instruments to promote multilateral sharing and common advocacy. Although declining, considerable sums are still channelled each year through the WCC to round-table and related multilateral programmes, making this the largest single programme area of the WCC's work.

In addition to long-term efforts, the Strategic Initiatives Fund (SIF) enables the WCC to respond to strategic or urgent needs of churches and ecumenical partners in the regions. In 2003, for example, over 25 projects were enabled in seven regions, ranging from support for the participation of Liberian church representatives in peace negotiations to the organization of an ecumenical delegation to Haiti as well as support for a new network of churches involved in anti-trafficking work in Eastern Europe.

In today's funding environment, the need to demonstrate recognizable and quantifiable successes still provides a fundamental challenge to

ecumenical diakonia. Addressing root causes of poverty, injustice and conflict often requires long and slow processes of dialogue, advocacy and capacity-building in which progress may not be easy to describe in annual reports. The WCC continues to hold before the ecumenical family the larger priorities that need concerted and sustained effort by the international ecumenical fellowship.

Because of the WCC's accompaniment of churches in the regions, it is well placed to help the international fellowship respond to crisis situations including political and economic crises. For instance, the grave social and economic crisis in Argentina at the end of 2001 led to the resignation of three presidents in the midst

"It becomes evident that principles guiding the ecumenical movement must allow sharing to be a mutual experience among the partners... The ecumenical movement must continue as a trail-blazer in showing the world how cooperation can be a cornerstone of relationships in the global village, built on the foundations of respect, courtesy and communication."

Bishop Mvume Dandala, presiding bishop, Methodist Church of Southern Africa, WCC round table, April 2002

97

Up to 300 displaced Roma are housed in this temporary camp at a former bus depot in north Mitrovice, Kosovo.

"It is not for us to analyze the causes of this crisis, which you know only too well. Let us simply say that the situation challenges us to continue our ethical and spiritual reflection on the role and behaviour of political leaders, international financial institutions and the different sectors of society. It also gives us cause to reflect further on our own commitment to action for life, justice and solidarity."

Rev. Dr Konrad Raiser,
in a letter to the churches in Argentina, January 2002

98

of massive and often violent popular unrest. Staff kept in constant contact with the churches and ecumenical bodies there, and provided some financial support for their efforts. The general secretary sent a letter of support to the churches in January 2002. To coordinate the ecumenical response, the WCC convened a round table with partners in early April to assess long-term needs and possibilities of support.

The WCC sought to strengthen platforms of dialogue and decision-making on ecumenical diaconal priorities by establishing in 2003 a Commission of the Churches on Diakonia and Development as well as a Commission on Justice, Peace and the Integrity of Creation. These commissions in part replaced advisory groups that no longer matched the internal structure of the WCC.

They also provide a stronger platform where churches, specialized ministries and church-related organizations are represented and can explore different approaches to development and ecumenical priorities and action. Efforts have also been made so that commissions on diakonia, justice and international affairs meet together in order to exchange ideas and information, ensure integration and avoid duplication of work.

In addition, in February 2005, the WCC, ecumenical agencies and churches working in the field of relief and development called for the creation of a new international alliance of church-related organizations to address issues of poverty and injustice. WCC member churches and agencies have struggled for years to find a common instrument bringing

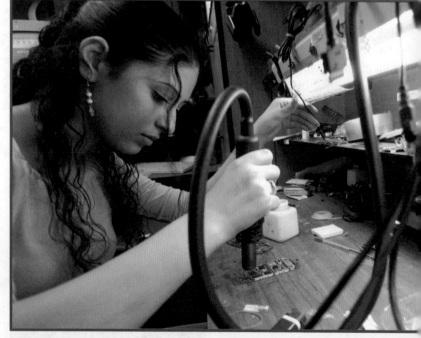

Rawa' Rabah, a graduate of an ACT-sponsored electronics training programme managed by the Lutheran World Federation in Beit Hanina, Palestine, works in a mobile phone shop in Ramallah.

together humanitarian relief, advocacy and development which can act quickly and flexibly. The WCC will play the central role in developing a provisional structure, negotiating with other ecumenical organizations involved in these areas, and perhaps initiating pilot projects.

WCC staff have also strengthened their cooperation with major secular international NGOs to improve service and humanitarian response, including the Pacific Partnership Forum, the ACP (Africa-Caribbean-Pacific) Civil Society Forum, the Steering Committee for Humanitarian Response, the International Council of Voluntary Agencies and the World Social Forum.

Staff represent the WCC in executive committee meetings of the United Nations High Commissioner for Refugees (UNHCR) and in the Inter-Agency Standing Committee (IASC) which brings together the directors of all UN agencies involved in humanitarian assistance. The WCC contributes to the development of international policies in UN organizations, NGO networks and civil society in the field of humanitarian response and development policy. Given the WCC's unique position as a global ecumenical body working in the field of development, diakonia and emergency response, the WCC provides a comprehensive context for the development of these policies.

Capacity-building and reflection on diakonia

One of the major goals of the WCC is to strengthen churches and ecumenical organizations to fulfil better their own missions, as well as to contribute to the ecumenical fellow-

99

An internally displaced Colombian woman earns money weaving in her home at the ACT-supported settlement near Neiva in Huila province.

Through regional desks, WCC programmes and priorities are communicated to churches in the regions and regional concerns are taken up at the global level.

The WCC has desks for Asia, Africa, Europe, Latin America and the Caribbean, the Middle East and the Pacific. A WCC office in New York has also provided a continuous WCC presence in the USA since even before the WCC was officially constituted.

The national and regional relationships fostered through regional desks provide a foundation for much of the work of the WCC in other programme areas. Regional staff have a comprehensive overview of developments and relationships in their respective regions. They link regional and international developments. They are often the key facilitators for visits by the WCC general secretary and other ecumenical delegations to different countries.

Each central committee meeting has a regional plenary in addition to issue-based plenaries, to review trends and challenges.

In 2003, two of the regional desks were relocated to the regions. The history of working through decentralized

(cont. on p.101)

ship. Churches and related organizations are becoming more aware of the need to equip themselves with new theoretical and practical tools to continue to fulfil their diaconal ministry in this rapidly changing and complex world – in short, to make the best use of their financial and human resources.

The capacity-building programme assists churches and related organizations at national, sub-regional and regional levels in leadership and management training, setting up finance and accounting systems, ecumenical formation, strategic planning, reporting and communication. Capacity-building also includes training in peace-building, conflict-resolution, advocacy and theological reflection.

The WCC first assists organizations in identifying needs for training and capacity-building, helps to develop training material in appropriate languages, and enables training in lead-

ership and organizational development. Workshops have been held for ecumenical and technical staff, women, youth and church leaders.

Undergirding discussions of funding and capacity-building are reflections on the mission of the churches in diakonia. Such theological and ethical reflections help elevate discussion from funding to partnership, justice and faithful stewardship. Churches and ecumenical organizations develop a more solid understanding of the theological basis for their work.

The WCC explores the links between diakonia and other elements in Christian life and witness, publishing findings in reports such as "Gender and Diakonia" and a study on the links between diakonia and justice.

Below: An ACT-sponsored carpentry workshop was part of the churches' response on behalf of thousands of Colombians who lost homes and jobs in a January 1999 earthquake. Right: A homeless person in the pews of St Martin in the Fields church, London.

Much of the capacity-building, reflection and solidarity efforts in diakonia are assisted by ecumenical enablers located in the regions. Enablers are identified by their professionalism and their commitment, out of their Christian faith, to work with poor and marginalized communities on a volunteer basis. Depending on the nature of cooperation, the enablers help represent the WCC at some regional meetings and their work is considered an extension of WCC regional programmes. At present, there are six enablers in Africa, three in the Pacific, three in Europe, seven in Latin America and the Caribbean, two in the USA and, with a broader definition, 22 in Asia.

Advocating for uprooted people

According to recent figures from the International Organization for Migration, there are 175 million migrants in the world, of whom 14 million are recognized refugees. An additional 20-25 million are internally displaced people.

The WCC provides ongoing opportunities for church partners working with these uprooted people to identify priorities and develop strategies appropriate to their regional contexts.

The WCC is a strong advocate at the international level for challenging national governments on their refugee and immigration policies and supporting adequate resourcing of international instruments, such as the UNHCR, that seek to assist and protect uprooted people.

Emphasis has also been placed on strengthening coordinated ecumenical actions on the issue of protection of refugees by advocating for the implementation of the UNHCR's Agenda for Protection, for appropriate responses to internally displaced people, for durable solutions for refugees who have lived in camps for

(cont. from p.100)

offices began with the WCC Office in the US, but in the past decade the Eastern European Office, the Ecumenical Women's Solidarity Fund and the Southeast Europe Ecumenical Partnership were created to respond to specific diaconal needs in different European contexts. In November 2002, the WCC officers decided to relocate the regional desks of the Pacific and the Middle East. The WCC office in the Pacific was opened in Suva, Fiji, in June 2003 and the WCC office in the Middle East was established in Beirut, Lebanon, in January 2004. The central committee in 2003 affirmed a process of review on the policy and effect of relocation to ensure "coherence and transparency".

Although each of the offices has its own unique characteristics and different mandates, they share the common characteristic that, by their very nature, they relate to many different teams and a wide range of ecumenical partners.

101

[Ecumenical enablers] see themselves not only as consultants but part of the ecumenical development. The path is sometimes very difficult and the willingness to carry the cross must be accepted... Enabling is still working in big ways. It is a burning passion which has to be completed.

WCC ecumenical enablers meeting, *November 2001*

many years, and for humane and liberal asylum policies.

Ecumenical regional networks have also been strengthened, and their capacity for information-sharing and implementation enhanced.

The WCC strengthened the Global Ecumenical Network on Uprooted People (GEN) to help link regional and national ecumenical networks of churches and agencies working with refugees and migrants in Africa, Asia, Australia, Canada, the Caribbean, Europe, Latin America, the Middle East, the Pacific and the USA. GEN serves as an advisory group to staff working on uprooted people and provides for joint assessment of trends, sharing of information, policy development and coordinated

actions on issues related to refugees, migrants and internally displaced persons. Representatives of Roman Catholic organizations, some Christian world communions, and United Nations organizations also participate in the meetings.

GEN meets annually in Geneva to review the global situation and future trends affecting uprooted people, to share information and to map out a common plan of action for the coming year. It meets immediately prior to the annual UNHCR meetings to enable participants to press their advocacy concerns with the UNHCR and participating governments.

Theological reflections on ministry with uprooted people are also shared with churches and ecumeni-

cal partners as a resource for individuals, churches and organizations.

The central committee in 2005 adopted a substantial memorandum on uprooted people which reflects on two of the last decade's disturbing developments in this field: the new patterns of migration as a result of globalization, and the effects of September 11 on the movement of people. Recalling the gospel imperative to practise hospitality towards strangers, the recommendations in the memorandum address international law and the role of governments, humanitarian considerations, detention and security, and the role of churches in monitoring and calling governments to be accountable for their treatment of migrants and asylum-seekers.

An external review of the WCC's advocacy work with the United Nations carried out in 2002 found that the Council's advocacy work on refugees, migrants and internally displaced people was one of the strongest areas of its engagement with the United Nations.

Supporting and involving children

A special programme on the dignity of children was established in 1995, responding to increasing numbers of orphans and children vulnerable to abuse and exploitation due to poverty, violence and HIV and AIDS. Three international consultations held between 1995 and 2000 encouraged the formation of networks where children themselves were active members and advocates. The WCC

Left: Two ethnic Hazara girls study in an ACT-supported Quetta school for Afghan refugees. Centre: In western Colombia, a woman and her child return from bathing in a settlement for those made homeless by the January 1999 earthquake. Right: A student at a youth training centre on the outskirts of Kampala, Uganda.

103

has facilitated the presence and participation of children in international forums, such as the United Nations tenth anniversary of the Convention on the Rights of the Child in 1999.

Regional consultations were then held in Africa, Asia, the Caribbean, Europe and Latin America "to empower churches in their ministry with children, especially marginalized children, and to develop appropriate regional approaches".

A mapping project of church actions with children in 14 countries in Asia was undertaken in 2003-2004 to improve networking and aid further discussions and action on the role of the church regarding children. As one result, churches in South Asia adopted an action plan in 2004 to help protect the rights of children and to

address issues such as child labour, a major concern in the region.

The WCC was one of the founding members of the Global Network of Religions for Children, which promotes the rights of children within their own religious traditions and across religious boundaries, cultures, economies, societies and families. Other networks are also supported in their work on human rights, development and children's issues such as the Ecumenical Disability Advocates Network (EDAN) and the Churches' Ministry with Children and Youth on Preventing Drug Addiction and HIV/AIDS Contamination.

The activities described in this chapter are the primary responsibility of the Diakonia and Solidarity staff team.

104

An Afghan boy works on a carpet in a vocational training school for refugees in Quetta, Pakistan.

Action by Churches Together (ACT) International

ACT was formed by the World Council of Churches and the Lutheran World Federation in 1995 to coordinate the international relief efforts of churches and their related agencies to victims of natural and environmental disasters, war and civil conflict. All the members of the WCC and LWF are eligible for membership in ACT. The number of ACT members active in emergency response has risen annually since its founding, indicating increased ecumenical collaboration in response to emergencies. The coordinating office is based at the Ecumenical Centre in Geneva.

For the period 1999-2003, ACT annually channelled between US$52 and 97 million in aid and relief efforts to humanitarian emergencies worldwide. ACT members contribute not only funds, but special expertise in areas such as de-mining, camp management, food and non-food distribution, health care and trauma counselling. ACT also conducts emergency management training in the field and administers rapid response funds to help alleviate immediate crises.

ACT's unique strength among relief organizations is its strong local roots through churches and related organizations within populations affected by emergencies. Thus ACT is able to provide locally based knowledge, analysis and understanding of emergencies.

A recent example of ACT's response through its local members is to the tsunami that devastated vast coastal

A grounded fishing ship in Indonesia, washed ashore during the Indian Ocean tsunami of 26 December 2004.

105

regions in south and southeast Asia on 26 December 2004. Within hours of the disaster, ACT members in the region, with the support of members of the alliance from around the world, were coordinating their emergency relief responses.

The greatest challenge is responding to "forgotten emergencies" – those not in the news headlines and often the result of ongoing and protracted conflict. For instance, in 1999 and 2000 the crisis in the Balkans region attracted more funding than any other

Year	Funding in USD	Number of countries
1999	$97 million	58
2000	$81 million	52
2001	$62.2 million	53
2002	$43.8 million	48
2003	$52.7 million	52
2004	$59.7 million	54

106

single emergency – yet at the same time critical human needs in countries like Sierre Leone, Congo and Afghanistan continued to be unmet and largely unnoticed by donors, from individuals to governments.

The WCC's work in advocacy for uprooted people complements ACT's work in emergency response. The WCC and the LWF are members of the Steering Committee for Humanitarian Response. The emergency network of the Catholic churches, Caritas Internationalis, is an observer on the ACT emergency committee. In a number of emergen-cies, ACT members work directly with UNHCR, the World Food Programme, UNICEF and other UN agencies.

ACT website: *http://act-intl.org/*

Below left: Following the tsunami, a woman sits amid the wreckage of her home in Maratuwa south of Colombo, Sri Lanka. Centre: A man surveys the wreckage of beachfront houses in Banda Aceh, Indonesia. Right: Shelters under construction to house 900 families whose homes were destroyed by the December 2004 tsunami, Tayagatha Pura Modra, Sri Lanka.

107

Ecumenical Church Loan Fund

The Ecumenical Church Loan Fund (ECLOF) is an ecumenical micro-finance network based in Geneva, Switzerland.

ECLOF makes small loans to groups of people for their micro-enterprises. Loans are also made to institutions for the construction of churches, schools and other community projects. Loans are made through national ECLOF committees in Africa, Asia and Latin America.

ECLOF loans are to poor and excluded groups who are committed to building sustainable livelihoods and communities, without discrimination with regard to religion or race, and to Christian-related organizations which do not otherwise have access to credit but who are committed to providing services or opportunities

for poor and excluded groups. It facilitates the sharing of resources that strengthen understanding, solidarity and self-reliance in ways that do not increase external indebtedness.

From 1998 to 2004, ECLOF made over 40,000 loans worth over US$84 million.

The WCC and ECLOF have a long history and special relationship. They work together in many areas and coordinate their programmes wherever possible. The WCC has two representatives on the ECLOF board.

ECLOF web site:
http://www.eclof.org/

A meeting of Banalata, a group of poor people of the village of Goharpur who are beneficiaries of the credit programme of the Christian Commission for Development in Bangladesh.

Upholding the Fullness of Life

The WCC's commitment in confronting economic globalization, environmental degradation and racism arises from its vision of abundant life for all. Lifting up the voices of Indigenous peoples, providing a platform for persons with disabilities, and empowering women at all levels of church and society often challenge the powerful and privileged while promoting justice and peace for all communities.

The ecumenical movement has long held a global vision of a world based on justice and peace, where the integrity of the earth is protected. Technological, economic and political forces have also had a profound global effect that often threatens such a vision. The Harare assembly stated that the challenges of economic globalization need to be placed at the centre of the ecumenical agenda.

Globalization is both a trend in the historical evolution of humanity and also a political ideology that encourages the market forces of global capitalism to direct the world's economy. For the ecumenical movement, globalization must be assessed against the goal of a life lived in dignity in just and sustainable communities. In the face of so much inequity, violence, and environmental and cultural destruction, the ecumenical move-

A social programme of the GMIN (Christian Evangelical Church in Minahasa) assists the families of garbage collectors at the local rubbish dump in Manado, North Sulawesi, Indonesia.

The logic of economic globalization is in opposition to the vision of the ecumenical movement of the unity of humankind and God's creation, the entire household of life. Lost is the understanding of the primacy of the dignity of the human person as made in the image of God, finding meaning in community. The underlying anthropology of economic globalization views humans as individuals rather than as persons in community, human beings as essentially competitive rather than cooperative, and human beings as materialist at the exclusion of the spiritual. Economic globalization threatens the diversity of cultures.

Central committee, *2001*

110

ment must develop alternatives, because the ecumenical movement itself, said the assembly, is "a different model of relationships, based on solidarity and sharing, mutual accountability and empowerment".

The central committee in 1999, in laying out the overarching foci of the WCC's work, recognized that globalization affects economic, political, ecological, cultural, social and religious life, and that the ecumenical movement must seek alternatives to the forces of globalization that are destructive, dividing and unjust. It is not just a "practical" problem – it is very much a theological and spiritual problem as well, and calls for the church to advocate for an "ethics of life".

Challenging global economic structures

The WCC works specifically on economic globalization through providing theological analysis, contributing to the global response, and developing and highlighting alternatives that call for full participation of all communities, especially those marginalized by poverty and disempowerment, in the development of trade and monetary policy and practices.

The WCC has followed closely a series of UN processes and institutions at the heart of the current global economic framework. In such processes, work is slow and almost always disappointing, but it has been vital to keep before government and policy representatives the critique and alternative vision in order to strengthen the position of those seeking a more just financial framework and to restrict further gains by powerful elites.

One such process was the United Nations general assembly Special Session on Social Development,

Cattle graze on the rubbish dump on the outskirts of Port-au-Prince, Haiti.

which met in Geneva in June 2000. The WCC and the Lutheran World Federation, through their offices in New York, followed preparations for this meeting for several years. Ecumenical delegations sent to the preparatory meetings gave ecumenical and grassroots input into the drafts and helped team members learn the UN system in order for them to be more effective advocates for their own communities. In selecting team members, priority was given to people from the South, to women and to Indigenous peoples, who have an expertise based on "lived experience".

It was clear that the ecumenical accompaniment of the long-term process made the ecumenical delegation one of the most organized and respected of the non-governmental advocates.

In a similar way, the WCC participated in the International Conference on Financing for Development held in Monterrey, Mexico, in 2002. Talking with government delegates, reporters and representatives of other non-governmental organizations, WCC representatives appealed for a more "people-centred approach" towards the alleviation of poverty and the democratization of such institutions as the World Bank, the International Monetary Fund and the World Trade Organization.

The WCC's dialogue with international monetary institutions has been approached with much caution. The WCC developed guidelines, "Lead Us Not into Temptation", on how churches can appropriately respond to invitations and engage in dialogue with the World Bank and the IMF. This responded to a central committee recommendation to develop

"As we cast our gaze ahead, we must work for another world, an alternative model of globalization and economic system...we need a fundamental collective change of heart to steer the course for our survival as a global community. This demands an alternative vision which does not reduce global interdependence to trade and markets."

Intervention at the Monterrey conference, on behalf of the ecumenical delegation, by Dr Molefe Tsele, general secretary, South Africa Council of Churches

111

A woman surveys the crops in Petite-Rivière, Haiti. ACT is working to counteract the effects of drought in the northwest of the island and to assist communities in need.

God, in your grac
transform the wor

World Council of Churche
9th Assembly
14-23 February 2006
Porto Alegre, Brazil

Members of the ecumenical coalition gather in Porto Alegre on the opening day of the World Social Forum, January 2005.

guidelines aiming for a consistent response from churches and ecumenical organizations to institutions promoting economic globalization.

From the perspective of the WCC and its concern for those living in poverty, the policies of the Bretton Woods institutions and the World Trade Organization have "not only failed to bridge the gap between rich and poor and achieve greater equality, but rather contributed to a widening gap". These policies, relying heavily on market forces, have virtually excluded the poor from any voice in social development or their own future and have brought social disintegration rather than development.

The WCC engaged in an intensive dialogue with the IMF and World Bank through three high-level encounters beginning in February 2003. These encounters culminated in October 2004 in a meeting between leaders from the three organizations: World Bank president James D. Wolfensohn, International

Monetary Fund deputy managing director Agustín Carstens, WCC general secretary Samuel Kobia and WCC president from Africa Agnes Abuom. The meeting emphasized that the three organizations find common ground in the fight against global poverty and the importance of the UN Millenium Development Goals, yet differ in areas such as approaches to development, financial markets and economic policy issues.

In articulating alternative visions and analysis to economic globalization, the WCC works together with the Lutheran World Federation, the World Alliance of Reformed Churches and the regional ecumenical organizations on consultations for theological reflections and analysis of the regional realities of globalization. Each of the organizations makes a distinct contribution to the dialogue on economic justice, with the WCC focusing on spiritual discernment as a basis for alternatives. Youth have been very involved in the consultations, both in their own forums and as integral partners in the consulta-

tions. These consultations have emphasized that partnership and mutual vulnerability are essential aspects of solidarity in the face of economic globalization.

From these ten regional consultations, with specific input from women and youth and the dialogue with international financial institutions, an ecumenical message on "Alternative Globalization Addressing People and Earth" (AGAPE) was drafted and shared with the churches for input before its submission to the ninth assembly in response to the Harare question: How do we live our faith in the context of globalization?

The WCC has been increasingly involved in the annual World Social Forum where it promotes ecumenical and interfaith cooperation in presenting alternatives to current models of economic globalization.

Such alternatives on a concrete level are developed and highlighted through the Ecumenical Coalition on Alternatives to Economic

Globalization, which is made up of the WCC, the Lutheran World Federation, the World Alliance of Reformed Churches, the World YWCA, the World Alliance of YMCAs, the World Student Christian Federation, Pax Romana and Frontier Internship in Mission. In seminars and forums, participants from different regions share thoughts and methodologies on alternative agriculture and equitable trade for small-scale farmers throughout the world. Exchanges are facilitated with those currently practising alternative agriculture and trade.

Women and economy

The WCC has attempted to point out that economic growth as prescribed by the world's dominant financial policy-makers has only worsened the condition of women. Poverty has a feminine face – research and studies have shown that economic globalization does not affect women and men in the same way. Because of differences in economic roles and longstanding imbalances in social status,

World Bank president James Wolfensohn, WCC general secretary Samuel Kobia and IMF managing director Rodrigo de Rato meet at the Geneva high level encounter, October 2004.

113

women – whether in developed or in developing countries – have a more negative experience with globalization in comparison with the rest of society. Overall, globalization processes have been associated with the feminization of labour, migration and even survival. The economic policies advocated by the International Monetary Fund and the World Bank, and the stabilizing and austerity measures taken, have worsened conditions, halting and even erasing some of the gains made in social welfare benefits such as health care and provision, education, nutrition and even income levels of women. Structural adjustment policies are largely formulated without any calculation of the imbalance of power in a patriarchal world order which often leads to the exclusion of women from the benefits of development and also attempts to silence women's strategies of resistance.

Yet women are not just victims. Women have historically adjusted to deprivation and demonstrated an extraordinary capacity for dealing with day-to-day problems of exclusion and poverty in imaginative yet practical ways. Therefore, a consultant from the Philippines, working on women and the economy, has developed a network of women economists and church women and has conceived a feminist ethic to enrich the discourse on alternatives to economic globalization. The model of a caring economy was also developed by this network.

With support from ACT International, women grow food for their families in the resettlement village of Bundas, Angola.

114

The WCC works further on issues of global trade through the Ecumenical Advocacy Alliance (see p. 125).

The difference
a letter can make

Activists are often dismayed – and sometimes rightly so – at the churches' predilection for making statements and writing letters in response to critical global events. And certainly, statements on their own mean nothing if not backed by moral leadership and action.

But sometimes, the effect of a letter can surprise even the letter writer.

During the United Nations general assembly Special Session on Social Development, which met in Geneva in June 2000, the ecumenical delegation that had followed the process were dismayed when UN secretary general Kofi Annan endorsed the position of the World Bank, the IMF

and the Organization for Economic Cooperation and Development in the report, A Better World for All, *which was issued on the opening day of the session.*

WCC general secretary Konrad Raiser sent Annan a letter, released to the press, reporting "great astonishment, disappointment and even anger" among many representatives of civil society that Annan had participated in "a propaganda exercise for international finance institutions whose policies are widely held to be at the root of many of the most grave social problems facing the poor". Noting the WCC's long-standing support of the principles of governance at the heart of the UN and personal support of Annan's leadership, Raiser said that Annan's

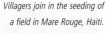

Villagers join in the seeding of a field in Mare Rouge, Haiti.

"One of the ecumenical movement's mandates is to be in solidarity with the poor; a clear response to the great commission given us by Jesus Christ to preach the good news to the poor, the good news that sets the captives free and proclaims the year of the Lord. Wherever forces of darkness, of death, have threatened life, the ecumenical movement has stood up to condemn, to speak and act against. In this particular moment, one of the manifestations of the forces of death to humanity, to life in its wholeness, is precisely the way economic management is being undertaken globally."

Agnes Abuom,
WCC president for Africa, Global Conference on Economic Globalization, Fiji, 2001

115

Left: A market in Suva, Fiji. Right: The market in Stepanakert, Nagorno-Karabagh.

willingness to put the UN on a partnership level with financial institutions controlled by a few highly industrialized countries damaged "the credibility of the UN as the last real hope of the victims of globalization".

Raiser admitted later that the letter produced "an unexpectedly wide echo". Extensively picked up in the media, it prompted Annan to reply quickly, and to release his letter to the press. This was the first time a UN general secretary has done so in correspondence with the WCC. It also awoke officials in the leading international financial institutions to the strong critique of the WCC. Officials at the IMF then sought a meeting with WCC leaders to discuss the points raised, which has led further to a series of encounters between the WCC, the IMF and the World Bank that look not only at trade and economic policy but at the fundamental principles of representation and governance which guide the organizations involved.

Ecological justice

While advocacy specifically on climate change has been an important activity of the WCC and the churches since the late 1980s, under the foci of "caring for life" the approach has been broadened not only to look at other issues, but to make links particularly between the environment and the economy. In 2001, the central committee also requested further work on addressing the responsibility of industrialized countries, encouraging churches in better stewardship and use of resources, and monitoring intergovernmental negotiations.

At the World Summit on Sustainable Development in Johannesburg in 2002, the WCC underlined that ecological responsibility cannot be seen in isolation from economic realities. The failure of the International Conference on Financing for Development in Monterrey to produce significant resources for assistance greatly hampered the potential of Johannesburg to deal effectively with ecological issues.

Three annual consultations and studies on theology of life and the environment culminated in an event in May 2005 in Basel, Switzerland, in combination with the assembly of the European Christian Environmental Network. Churches' initiatives and activities were presented that linked economic justice and environmental concerns, including the concept of ecological debt.

The central committee in 2001 and 2002 also acted on the need for the implementation of the Kyoto Protocol of the UN Framework Convention on Climate Change. The WCC attended all the meetings of the Conference of Parties (COP) of the UN Framework Convention on Climate Change (UNFCCC), with increasing interfaith participation and cooperation in the monitoring process, along with a newly formed group of Indigenous peoples' communities. The WCC sponsored interfaith colloquiums and ecumenical workshops at the event, and called attention to changes in government policies requiring an ethical and spiritual response. The UN secretariat for the UNFCCC has publicly expressed admiration for the WCC's consistent and helpful work during the climate-change negotiations. The WCC celebrated the enforcement of the Kyoto Protocol on 16 February 2005 as a symbol that solidarity between nations and people is not only needed but possible, against all odds and the opposition of very powerful countries.

The WCC participates in such forums primarily by bringing people from different regions with local and specific expertise and experience. The WCC is also informed through regional and issue-based consultations. Work with the churches in the Pacific has been particularly important. Youth and women's meetings, in addition to consultations with church representatives and environmental experts over several years, have identified important links between globaliza-

Forest fires in Guatemala have forced farmers from certain lowlands, leading them to occupy ecologically fragile hillsides.

117

Left: A tree is chopped down in Haiti, adding to the nation's struggle with deforestation. Right: A Colombian child bathes in an ACT-supported settlement for the internally displaced.

tion and global warming, with the potential to devastate the entire region.

The WCC supported the formation of the Network on Climate Change and Water as a platform for cooperation and common action between different partners in the ecumenical movement and beyond. The network contributed to the World Social Forum and helped to focus public advocacy against the privatization of goods essential for life, i.e. water.

Work on genetic engineering has also gained increasing attention in the WCC, particularly at the meeting of the central committee in 2003 in relation to the concerns and activities of the Ecumenical Disability Advocates Network (EDAN) and of Indigenous peoples. Churches are not only challenged by the scientific and technological developments as such, but also by the commercial applications of science that have intensified the commodification of life.

In addition to contributing to the debate on intellectual property rights and working with farmers' communities on agriculture and seed varieties, the WCC continues to monitor the issue of food aid and genetically modified organisms in cooperation with Action by Churches Together (ACT) International, APRODEV and Friends of the Earth. Support was given to national initiatives, e.g. by the South African Council of Churches.

An ecumenical platform for exchange of information, reflection and common action on issues related to genetic engineering has developed in response to a recommendation by the WCC central committee, along with a study document prepared for the churches.

Working in solidarity with Indigenous peoples

The need for "inclusive community" was highlighted at the Harare assembly, not least in relation to Indigenous peoples. The assembly

heard a challenge from a pre-assembly meeting of Indigenous peoples that much more work needs to be done by churches and by the WCC – in dialogue, in respect, in solidarity with Indigenous peoples.

The WCC has worked to raise justice and identity issues between Indigenous peoples and the churches, to facilitate a dialogue of Indigenous spiritualities with Christianity and other religions, and to affirm ancestral knowledge, identity and contributions to caring for the earth and for future generations.

In his visit to Bolivia in November 2004, Samuel Kobia emphasized that the spirituality of Indigenous peoples has a great deal to contribute to the Western cosmovision.

Indigenous peoples' perspectives and participation have been promoted in, particularly, debates on alternatives to globalization and work on racism. Exchanges of Indigenous church leaders have been encouraged nationally and regionally, and leadership training and capacity-building for church and community spiritual leaders supported.

The WCC has also advocated for Indigenous peoples at the United Nations, particularly with the Working Group on Indigenous Peoples, which monitors developments and sets standards for governments to adopt, and also through supporting work on the draft Declaration on Indigenous Peoples' Rights. The WCC has been a strong advocate for a permanent forum on Indigenous issues, which was finally established in May 2002, to provide advice, raise awareness and coordinate activities within the UN system. The establishment of the forum has come after a long process begun when Indigenous peoples approached the League of Nations early in the 20th century. This very positive outcome is the result of unity and strong effort made by

Left: A woman carries water in Ganaives, Haiti. Right: Dancers celebrate the gift of life at the World Social Forum, Porto Alegre, Brazil, January 2003.

119

Fishermen on the Brhmaputa River in northern Bangladesh.

Indigenous peoples in different processes towards the forum.

The WCC has facilitated meetings of Indigenous representatives and provided resources for their participation in UN forums. The Ecumenical Centre in Geneva has become a home for Indigenous representatives during their participation in many UN sessions and their meetings with UN officials. The WCC has traditionally hosted a preparatory meeting to the UN fora at the Ecumenical Centre, usually attended by around 200 delegates.

In 2004, the WCC delegation called on the UN to sponsor an International Year of Indigenous Languages in 2006 in recognition that three-quarters of the world's linguistic diversity is found among Indigenous peoples and that, according to UNESCO, one language is lost about every two weeks. In 2005, the central committee urged the estab-

lishment of a UN International Year of Indigenous Languages as well as the signing of the UN Declaration on the Rights of Indigenous Peoples.

In 2003, as the WCC's financial crisis created impetus to look at new ways of working, the office for Indigenous peoples was decentralized, moving to Latin America in collaboration with the Latin American Council of Churches. The executive committee affirmed "working closely with member churches and ecumenical organizations, making joint appointments wherever possible", but emphasized that the WCC maintains its commitment to Indigenous peoples as part of its core programme.

Proclaiming a church for all: Ecumenical Disability Advocates Network

The interim theological statement presented to the central committee in 2003 (see p.47) came out of work by and with persons with disabilities. Disabilities has been on the agenda of the WCC since the early 1980s, but the Harare assembly was the springboard for creation of the Ecumenical Disability Advocates Network (EDAN) to support the work of individuals, churches and organizations to improve the space for all people in the life of the church.

EDAN has worked on issues of education for clergy and lay training, as well as facilitating regional networking and awareness-building seminars. The international coordination office is located in Nairobi, Kenya.

The WCC is committed to supporting the network in creative ways, enabling the participation of persons with disabilities in advisory groups and governing bodies, and incorporating the concerns from the network in ongoing activities.

Broadening definitions and response to racism
The United Nations World Conference on Racism held in Durban in 2001 became a pivotal point for the ecumenical movement in noting progress – and lack thereof – on historical concerns and definitions of racism as well as new manifestations of racial intolerance, xenophobia and discrimination which exist in virtually every society.

To prepare for the world conference, the WCC facilitated regional meetings in Latin America and the Spanish-speaking Caribbean, North

America, Asia/Pacific and Africa. The major concerns reported in the gatherings made a significant contribution to the debate on new manifestations of racism in today's global society. A dossier based on the work of the regional meetings, "Understanding Racism Today", was prepared in time for the world conference.

The extensive consultation process resulted in a large WCC delegation attending the NGO forum, including representatives of the Sinti and Roma peoples, Palestinians, Dalits,

More than 40,000 people – most of them Dalits and Indigenous people – live in Kusumpur, one of many slums surrounding Delhi, India.

121

Archbishop Desmond Tutu of South Africa, Nobel laureate for peace, speaks in Geneva on the 50th anniversary of the World Council of Churches, 22 September 1998.

women, youth, Africans and people of African descent, Indigenous peoples and other minority groups. WCC representatives remained in Durban for the intergovernmental conference. Archbishop Desmond Tutu's presence at the press conference organized by the ecumenical caucus put the churches on the front page of many newspapers.

The WCC noted that discussions at the world conference gave new impetus to the quest to understand restorative and transformative justice. As WCC staff remarked, "It is no longer sufficient merely to record past injustices. We must search for ways to restore the lives and dignity of those who were victims."

This resonated with a concern coming from the Africa and Asia regional groups within the central committee in 2001 about the ongoing and intensified experience of racism and xenophobia in Europe. The WCC in

2001 conducted research into church-sponsored initiatives dealing with racism and xenophobia in Great Britain, France, Germany and Austria.

The central committee participated in a plenary session on racism in 2002. The report "Being Church and Overcoming Racism: It Is Time for Transformative Justice" reviewed recent experiences of corporate confession and conversion from racist practices among WCC member churches, including the United Church of Canada, the United Methodist Church in the US, the Lutheran Church of Norway and the churches of South Africa. The report recognized that there is no magic formula for the church and society to seek "transformative justice" – the renewal of minds and hearts to establish more just relationships.

A resource guide entitled *Transformative Justice: Being Church and Overcoming Racism* was pro-

Dalit protestors at the UN World Conference against Racism, demonstrating against their government's refusal to equate casteism with discrimination. Durban, South Africa, September 2001.

duced in 2004. The central committee commended this study document to the churches and asked that a review be undertaken in order to provide input for the ninth assembly.

In other areas of the WCC's work on racism, the Women under Racism Programme (WURP) facilitated encounters between black, Indigenous and ethnic minority women to share their life experiences, their particular struggles, analysis of their own situation and their dreams and strategies for future follow-up. The programme has broadened the opportunity of developing theological reflection and other materials from race, gender and class perspectives, for use in congregations and church-related women's groups.

The Special Fund to Combat Racism continues to include small grants to organizations actively opposing racism.

Women's voices and visions

The Ecumenical Decade in Solidarity with Women concluded in Harare, but the assembly encouraged churches to keep before them the goals of the Decade. Efforts to give women a voice in crit-ical society developments as well as in the church, to respond to women facing violence, to assist women in leadership development, and to document and recognize the contributions of women in ecumenical life and the church have been a vibrant part of the WCC's activities since Harare.

The study and reflection process on "Women's Voices and Visions on Being Church" is a follow-up of the ecclesiological challenges from the Ecumenical Decade. The process documents women's ways and visions of being church by affirming alternatives to the present structures which deny the presence and full participation of women. Issues such as violence against women and the use and abuse of power in the churches were addressed. A series of regional meetings of women theologians were held in collaboration with regional ecumenical organizations (Asia 2001; Latin America 2002; Africa 2003; North America 2004; Europe 2005). Orthodox women as well as young women made a special contribution to the process.

A steering group accompanied the process, drawing together all the reflections

123

Candlelight march following the ecumenical service at the UN World Conference against Racism, from Central Methodist church to city hall. Durban, South Africa, September 2001.

and preparing the final report and documentation to be shared at the ninth assembly. Resource materials are being produced, some in collaboration with regional ecumenical organizations, and made available to women in the networks.

The WCC also assisted women from Africa, Asia and Latin America to participate in leadership development through various outlets including the UN Commission on the Status of Women, leadership training programmes and research seminars. By enabling the participation of women in UN processes, the role of Christian women and the issues of religion and women are enhanced.

Violence against women became a focus of critical attention in resources produced by DOV and special campaigns in which the WCC participated. Working through the Christian world communions, and with an office set up in Edinburgh, Scotland, the churches' responses to violence against women was monitored and a dossier of church responses prepared for the ninth assembly.

In addition to these specific efforts, concern for the inclusion of women's voices and visions is integrated across WCC activities – in theological study, mission approaches, response to conflict situations, education, economic justice and more.

(See also supporting participation and leadership of youth, page 29)

The activities described in this chapter are the primary responsibility of the Justice, Peace and Creation staff team

Chung Hyun Kung of Korea, one of more than a thousand women who participated in the celebration of the Ecumenical Decade Festival in Harare, 27-30 November 1998.

The symbol or logo of the Ecumenical Advocacy Alliance, an instrument for common action on the issues of global trade and HIV/AIDS.

Ecumenical Advocacy Alliance

Conversations about new ways of doing common advocacy work between the WCC and development agencies, along with other churches and ecumenical organizations beyond the WCC fellowship, intensified after the Harare assembly. Looking at successful models of how civil society had mobilized on issues such as climate change and landmines, the desire was to set up a flexible, coordinating instrument to work together on a few issues commonly defined as priorities.

The WCC facilitated the founding meeting of the Ecumenical Advocacy Alliance which was held in December 2000. Out of over one hundred suggested issues, global trade and HIV/AIDS were named as foci for common advocacy, along with a special concentration on networking and information-sharing for peace and conflict resolution.

The Ecumenical Advocacy Alliance has brought together more than 85 churches and church-related organizations as participants, from small churches, Christian world communions, church-related agencies and organizations outside of the WCC fellowship such as Franciscans International.

Strategy groups for HIV/AIDS and global trade were set up which developed a plan of action for each of the two foci over a 3-4 year period. The WCC was part of both strategy groups, as well as a permanent member of the governing body of the Alliance, the ecumenical advocacy committee.

The HIV/AIDS campaign "I Care, Do You? The Churches Say Yes!" was launched in 2001 with advocacy goals in four areas: eradicating stigma and discrimination; working for effective prevention by addressing root causes of vulnerability; promoting access to treatment, including antiretroviral drugs; and lobbying governments, intergovernmental organizations and others to mobilize enough resources to combat the pandemic effectively.

125

"If you don't see a difference, don't invent one!" Winning Portuguese entry in a global poster competition sponsored by EAA to combat HIV/AIDS stigma and discrimination. Artist: Carlos Edgar Costa

Se não, vê diferenças...
HIV-   *HIV +*
Não as invente!

TRADE FOR
Global
Campaign
PEOPLE

The symbol of the EAA's "Trade for People" campaign for a just pattern of fair trading among both rich and poor.

A global petition was used to raise awareness in local and national campaigns, advocacy and educational resources were compiled and shared, worship and biblical reflection material was developed, and assistance was given in coordinating ecumenical efforts such as at the World Social Forum.

In April 2005, the Alliance mobilized wide church-based participation in the global week of action on trade to raise worldwide awareness of the concerns for trade justice and impress upon policy-makers the combined strength of the global trade justice campaigns.

Under its special concern for peace and reconciliation, the Ecumenical Advocacy Alliance helped set up the "Behind the News" electronic information service with the WCC and ACT International to share alternative, faith-based news and analysis on countries and regions of world concern.

After an outside evaluation of the Alliance a second assembly of participants and interested organizations, held in November 2004, reaffirmed the EAA as a common instrument for advocacy and voted to continue its emphases on global trade and HIV and AIDS over the next four years.

Ecumenical Advocacy Alliance website: *http://www.e-alliance.ch/*

One of its most successful endeavours was the global poster competition against HIV- and AIDS-related stigma and discrimination. A CD-Rom, "Signs of Hope, Steps for Change", contained winning posters and over one hundred other multilingual and multimedia resources to support churches and community groups in continuing the dialogue about HIV- and AIDS-related stigma and discrimination.

The Alliance also took the lead in facilitating ecumenical cooperation at the international AIDS conference in Bangkok in 2004, which raised the visibility of faith-based efforts to combat HIV and AIDS.

Global trade proved a far more complex topic on which to reach common agreement on advocacy. The "Trade for People" campaign was launched in 2002 to call for the recognition that human rights and social and environmental agreements take priority over trade agreements and policies.

Promoting Peace, Security and Human Rights

From the NATO bombing of Kosovo to the attacks of 11 September 2001 and the war in Iraq, the WCC has responded pastorally and prophetically to challenge the use of violence, uphold human rights, resolve conflict and build true security. All these issues have been especially acute in Israel and Palestine, where the WCC and ecumenical partners have accompanied both sides in pursuit of sustainable peace with justice.

"Truth, justice and peace together represent values basic to granting of human rights, inclusion and reconciliation," said the Harare assembly's programme guidelines committee. "When these values are ignored, trust is replaced by fear and human power no longer serves the gift of life and the sanctity and dignity of all in creation."

Part of the WCC's central role is to call attention to situations of injustice or conflict, enable churches and ecumenical partners to develop meaningful and active witness on international political concerns, and promote coherent and common ecumenical approaches to world problems. Through the Commission of the Churches on International Affairs

When the WCC acts on international affairs, it is as a fellowship of churches who live and witness in a wide variety of social, economic, political and ideological situations. Their possibilities of actions and the problems they face differ widely. History, tradition, culture and the present circumstances must all be taken into account. Public actions of the WCC must be characterized by a sensitivity to the special needs of each church and its context.

127

(cont. on page 128)

A protestor decorates the Israeli separation wall while soldiers await orders to direct their response in the face of this non-violent activity.

(cont. from page 127)

Under certain circumstances, the WCC hears conflicting voices coming from the churches in a particular place. In addition the assessment made from a global perspective may differ from a national one. When such differences occur care must be taken about the possible effect of WCC action. Disagreements do arise from time to time between a church or group of churches and the international body. These need not be avoided for the sake of harmony within the fellowship, but rather must be accepted as a necessary consequence of exercising the obligation of discernment as well as that of mutual challenge for renewal in the spirit of the fellowship.

*From **The Role of the World Council of Churches in International Affairs**, 1999*

128

(CCIA), this has been a core task of the ecumenical fellowship even prior to the official formation of the WCC.

Response to conflict

The WCC has long facilitated the work of the churches in tense situations in hopes of resolving crises before violence erupts, in the midst of armed conflict and war, and in its aftermath, in helping people rebuild their lives and establish a just and sustainable peace.

To do this, the WCC promotes efforts at mediation, conflict transformation, just peace-making and reconciliation through pastoral visits to churches and national officials, capacity-building activities, advocacy through confidential representations to governments, public statements and appeals, studies and reports by ecumenical teams of observers, ecumenical delegations, and constant monitoring, analysis and interpretation.

The WCC's actions are guided by policy statements established by its governing bodies. Underlying all is the biblical vision of peace with justice so that all may experience "life in all its fullness".

The major international conflicts of the last seven years are tragic reminders of how far the world is from that biblical vision.

Kosovo crisis

Soon after the Harare assembly, the fellowship of churches was called to respond to the mass exodus of Kosovar Albanians, following a period of civil conflicts, the NATO air campaign against Serbia and Montenegro, and then the return of the refugees to often decimated towns and villages under an uneasy truce monitored by UN forces. The WCC expressed its profound concerns about the rights of minorities and condemned the violence on all sides that added further

The funeral of a Palestinian youth killed in the violence of the intifada, East Jerusalem.

bloodshed and instability in a troubled region since the break-up of the former Yugoslavia.

The WCC closely coordinated its response to the Kosovo crisis with the Conference of European Churches, the Lutheran World Federation and the World Alliance of Reformed Churches, all based in the Ecumenical Centre in Geneva. International relief was channelled through Action by Churches Together (ACT) International, with the Orthodox Autocephalous Church of Albania playing a key role.

In addition to advocacy through letters and meetings with European and international officials, the WCC expressed pastoral support through prayers, letters and visits to the affected region.

In May 1999, an international ecumenical consultation brought togeth-er some forty church leaders from Europe and North America, including representatives from four churches in Yugoslavia – Lutheran, Methodist, Reformed and Serbian Orthodox – as well as from the Council of European [Catholic] Bishops Conferences, who insisted that the United Nations and the Organization for Security and Cooperation in Europe should play a central role in negotiations. Such meetings demonstrate the unique space the WCC can create in bringing churches from all the countries involved together for dialogue and action.

September 11, 2001

News on September 11, 2001 was brought immediately to the WCC executive committee then meeting in Geneva. A pastoral letter was drafted and sent within hours to the US churches assuring them of the prayers of the worldwide church. A "Living Letters" delegation was

A member of Israel's "Women in Black" protests the occupation of Palestinian territories in the group's weekly peace vigil in Jerusalem.

It is always difficult to walk into a house of grief. But you have received us with gracious hospitality in this time of sorrow, and we are grateful. In South Africa, there is a saying used at the time of mourning: "What has happened to you has happened to others as well." We are witnesses that God makes it possible for life to continue. Many American churches have visited us in our difficult times to help us find a way when we have been overwhelmed with our grief. We now say to you, take courage. We have come to you as living letters, signs of hope in the suffering and pain of the cross.

Message from the ecumenical
"Living Letters"
delegation to US churches,
November 2001

130

sent to the US churches in November 2001. The delegation members came from South Africa, France, Pakistan, Russia, Indonesia, Lebanon and Palestine and were accompanied by the WCC president from the US and the WCC deputy general secretary.

The team went to New York, Chicago and Washington DC, ending their visit at the National Council of the Churches of Christ annual meeting in Oakland, California. The expression of international concern and solidarity and members' personal experience of violence and hope provided a powerful expression of the international fellowship of churches.

An alternative electronic information service, "Behind the News: Visions for Peace – Voices of Faith" was created jointly by the WCC, ACT International and the Ecumenical Advocacy Alliance. "Behind the News" featured church and ecu-

menical statements, messages and actions from other faiths, humanitarian updates, analysis, resources and worship suggestions on situations of global concern. The bulletins highlighted the ability of the WCC to bring many areas of expertise to bear on an issue, to assess and analyze inputs and events from global and regional perspectives, and to improve communication and sharing among the constituency.

Through ACT International, churches responded to the fighting in Afghanistan. ACT member agencies had been operating in the country long before the events of 2001. By the end of the year, ACT was mobilizing efforts to aid refugees in and around the war-torn nation.

Israel-Palestine
Since 1948 the WCC has been working on the Israeli-Palestinian conflict. It has closely monitored negotiations,

At the outbreak of conflict in Kosovo in the spring of 1999, more than 300,000 refugees were settled in tent camps around the Albanian capital of Tirana.

repeatedly called for the implementation of United Nations resolutions, and supported local churches in efforts to build bridges of peace and reconciliation between the two communities and engage in non-violent action to end the occupation.

Since the Harare assembly, the WCC has engaged much more intensively in advocating for a comprehensive peace agreement and efforts for a lasting peace with justice. The WCC governing bodies have adopted more statements on the Arab-Israeli conflict between the assemblies of Harare (1998) and Porto Alegre (2006) than between Amsterdam (1948) and Harare.

The start of the second Intifada in September 2000 intensified ecumenical efforts to support local peace initiatives and demand a return to negotiations. To express solidarity, and to listen carefully to local churches and respond to their analysis and needs in the critical situation, the WCC facilitated several ecumenical and staff visits to Jerusalem and the Occupied Palestinian Territories, meeting with church leaders, Palestinian and Israeli peace and human-rights activists, and political leaders on both sides.

An ecumenical campaign was endorsed by the WCC executive committee as part of the Decade to Overcome Violence that called upon the churches to "focus attention in 2002 on intensive efforts to end the illegal occupation of Palestine". A video prepared as part of the campaign, "Ending Occupation: Voices for a Just Peace", features interviews with local church and religious leaders and Palestinian and Israeli human-rights activists, who outline the root causes of violence in the region as well as opportunities for a just peace.

"What one has seen after September 11 is that tolerance and respect among peoples, which are foundational tenets of the charter of the United Nations, must now become crucial components of future security strategies. A world in which one group feels that it is being looked down upon by another is a world that will remain insecure. The assault on poverty is an integral part of the quest for dignity, equality, respect and decent life-chances in the world. Global security would simply not be possible in a world of increasing poverty."

B.G. Ramcharan, *Deputy High Commissioner for Human Rights, United Nations - Geneva Office, speaking at a WCC consultation, "Beyond September 11: Assessing the Global Implications", 2001*

131

Left: Kosovar refugees in a church-supported camp near Krume, Albania, 1999. Right: Albanian schoolboys herd their families' goats.

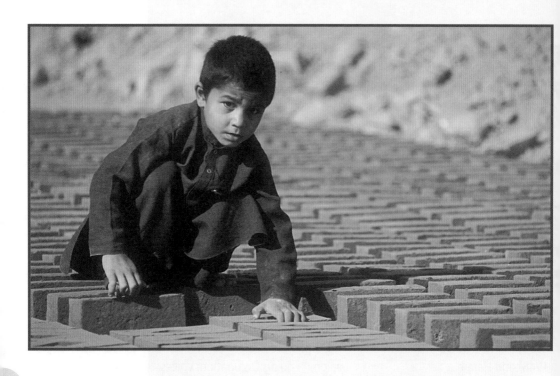

In October 2001, a young Afghan refugee makes bricks near the Shamshatoo refugee camp in Pakistan.

As the oppression and violence escalated in the region, more direct action was required, and the WCC with key ecumenical partners set up the Ecumenical Accompaniment Programme in Palestine and Israel (EAPPI) (see p.141).

In 2005, the WCC central committee encouraged the WCC's member churches "to give serious consideration to adopting measures that avoid participating economically in illegal activities related to the Israeli occupation". In that sense, the committee affirmed "economic pressure, appropriately and openly applied" as a "means of action" and a way to work for peace in this conflict.

The WCC, after a comprehensive consultative process with the heads of churches in Jerusalem and the Middle East Council of Churches, also established in 2005 a Jerusalem ecumenical centre in the old city to serve as a focal point for church witness in Jerusalem and advocacy in the region.

Iraq

In September 2002, in response to growing global tension concerning Iraq, the central committee warned the US and UK governments against a pre-emptive invasion of Iraq and called instead for the international rule of law to be upheld and efforts by the UN security council for non-military means to resolve the crisis to be strengthened.

Continued threats of military action brought growing unanimity among church members around the world opposing military action and supporting more consideration and emphasis on non-military solutions.

The WCC convened an international meeting of church leaders in Berlin in February 2003 who stressed their "spiritual obligation, grounded in God's love for all humanity, to speak out against war in Iraq". The WCC executive committee followed a few weeks later with a strong statement opposing war in Iraq and voicing deep concerns for the humanitarian and long-term consequences of such an action. The call to the churches to join in a day of prayer for peace in Iraq at the beginning of Lent was widely covered in the media, reflecting the unique contribution of churches in a potentially religiously polarized conflict. On 20 March, when the war on Iraq started, the general secretary of the World Council of Churches, Konrad Raiser, stated the pre-emptive strike was immoral, illegal and ill-advised.

The WCC worked closely with the Middle East Council of Churches in monitoring the regional situation and enabling church statements to be translated into Arabic and distributed widely. Partners in the Middle East credited such efforts with minimizing Christian-Muslim tensions during the crisis.

The continued instability and violence in the country remain a deep concern, leading to the central committee stating in 2005 that "the crisis in Iraq persists at the expense of the Iraqi people and with long-term complications for the international community". "Regrettably" reaffirming positions the WCC had taken in the previous three years, the central committee renewed calls for accountability to international law by governments and intergovernmental bodies, a timetable for the reduction and

A Palestinian boy tends his family's olive grove near Ti'innik on the West Bank.

133

"When we deal with the churches, the key word is diversity: historically, theologically, spiritually. Yet when it comes to injustice, human rights and peace, there is not a Greek Orthodox answer, a Catholic answer, an Armenian Orthodox answer. There is a Christian answer. Palestinians, whether they are Muslims or Christians, are victims of huge injustice and are struggling for peace. Our answer is that any peace based on injustice will never last."

Jerusalem church representative, *EAPPI, February 2002*

134

removal of US coalition forces, and a greater role for the United Nations in helping the Iraqi people to gain effective control of their country.

Regional conflicts

The WCC was a strong advocate in addressing human-rights abuses and religious tensions in Indonesia and East Timor. Delegations and appeals to the government about the violence and continuing impunity for leaders of the security forces who had committed "grave abuses of human rights" were part of the ecumenical response. Raiser visited Indonesia in 2000 and met with president Abdurrahman Wahid. Such visits and public statements also press upon political and religious leaders that the international community is aware and attentive to the situation in the country.

The WCC helped to support interfaith peace efforts in West Africa, in cooperation with the All Africa Conference of Churches and the subregional fellowship. A consultation in April 2001 which brought together interfaith coun-

cils from the Côte d'Ivoire, Guinea, Liberia and Sierra Leone was a landmark effort that highlighted the willingness, commitment and capacity of the religious leaders to deal with conflict situations in a collaborative spirit, and shows the potential of religious leaders to make a difference in complicated political issues (See also the Focus on Africa, p.144)

WCC efforts to bring peace and reconciliation between North and South Korea began in the 1980s when the WCC enabled church leaders from North and South to meet together for the first time since the country was divided. In 1999, Konrad Raiser was the first WCC general secretary to visit North as well as South Korea.

Right: Palestinian students on their way to school in Hebron as they approach a military checkpoint. Above, opposite: Two ecumenical accompaniers approach an Israeli checkpoint on the main road into Jenin, Palestine, August 2004.

At the 2004 executive committee meeting in Seoul, Moderator Aram I recognized the prophetic role of churches in Korean unity and peace. A statement called for actions reinforcing stability, dialogue and exchange in the region.

A consultation held in Tozanzo, Japan, in October 2004 brought together church representatives from North and South Korea to debate issues of peace and reunification.

Support for confidence-building measures between churches in India and Pakistan aimed at overcoming violence and encouraging both sides to work towards the denuclearization and demilitarization of the region. A meeting with the religious communities of the Former Yugoslav Republic of Macedonia, held in

Morges, Switzerland, 11-13 June 2001, led to the signing of an agreement aimed at stabilizing inter-religious cooperation after an eruption of violence in the country that reflected the instability of the region.

The WCC has facilitated a common ecumenical policy and response to the Cyprus problem, accompanying the Church of Cyprus and all those in civil society working on peace-building and reconciliation towards a reunified, federal and bi-communal solution.

Ecumenical peace efforts in Guatemala and Colombia strengthen the work of the churches in these countries to overcome violence and build just and peaceful societies. Visits provide solidarity, workshops strengthen the capacity of Christian leaders and other civil-society actors,

Reliance on military solutions to human problems and divisions persists and, in some ways, has grown. The consultation questioned the justice and value of human security based on military security. Solutions to conflicts too often rely on military power. But this cannot be the ultimate basis for people's security... From the perspective of faith, the security of all is judged by the shalom security of the poorest, the weakest, the excluded, the subjugated, the minjung...

Report of the Ecumenical Consultation on Justice, Peace and People's Security in Northeast Asia, February 2001

Left: "Water – a human right" demonstration at the 2003 World Social Forum. Centre: A woman at prayer in the Chaldean Catholic Church in Baghdad, Iraq.

and delegations are supported to advocate at international forums.

The central committee in 1999 examined the growing trend of using military interventions ostensibly on behalf of humanitarian causes, and commissioned the WCC to conduct a study on the ethics of humanitarian intervention. The study process on the responsibility to protect, highlighting ethical, political, legal and theological implications, continued in close collaboration with academic institutions and other ecumenical partners, with a final draft of this study prepared for the ninth assembly.

The WCC monitors other critical national and international situations, and advises and supports churches on appropriate responses. The Commission of the Churches on International Affairs, at its meeting in May 2004, recommended a particular focus on four different situations until the Porto Alegre assembly: Israel/Palestine, Korea, Zimbabwe and Cuba.

The CCIA, which comprises thirty people nominated by churches and regional ecumenical organizations, meets approximately every 18 months to advise staff and reflect on trends and needs in international affairs. Executive and central committees consider public issues at each meeting and receive background information and analysis from WCC staff on situations and issues that are being monitored and addressed, along with recommendations for response by the fellowship. A list of statements and minutes on public issues can be found in Appendix E on p.200.

Impunity and reconciliation

As part of its response to conflict, the WCC promotes awareness that issues of truth, justice, repentance, forgiveness and reconciliation are interconnected and necessary elements of sustainable peace.

The WCC has supported "truth and reconciliation" commissions that have been established in several countries, both observing and facilitating the

At the entrance to the chapel of the Ecumenical Centre in Geneva, candles are lit and prayers said for peace as the "shock and awe" bombardment of Iraq begins, 20 March 2003.

137

sharing of study resources and reports. In February 2003, the development of truth and reconciliation processes in various countries, especially in Peru and Sierra Leone, was examined by a panel at the World Social Forum in which the WCC highlighted the central role of churches and religious communities in these processes.

The WCC works on the ethical, theological, political and legal implications of impunity and the absence of accountability for human-rights violations and the path towards reconciliation through restorative justice. The WCC has warned against efforts to produce a too-easy "reconciliation" after a period of bloody dictatorship by granting impunity to government and military officials responsible for killings, torture, disappearances and other abuses. *Beyond Impunity: An Ecumenical Approach to Truth, Justice and Reconciliation*, published in English, French and Spanish, and "Restorative Justice: Selected Readings" serve as important study and reflection documents for churches and civil society.

The WCC highlights the need for justice and reconciliation in the international arena, including advocating for universal ratification of the International Criminal Court and the approval of a convention on forced disappearance. The central committee in 2005 adopted a statement on this issue.

Human rights

The WCC regularly monitors the status of human rights in critical situations around the world and promotes the capacity of churches, ecumenical organizations and networks to engage in advocacy at local, national and international levels.

The United Nations Commission on Human Rights meets annually in Geneva. The WCC, working closely with the Lutheran World Federation, the World Alliance of Reformed Churches, Franciscans International and the Dominicans, brings before the commission the churches' concerns on human rights.

Each year the WCC in cooperation with church partners makes written

"Knowing the truth about human-rights violations is one of the essential elements in coming to terms with the past and establishing the foundation for a possible reconciliation."

Rev. Dr Samuel Kobia, *during his visit to Uruguay, November 2004*

The churches are well placed to acknowledge and testify to the impact of small arms, since they minister to the victims and their families all around the world, in rich and poor nations. Churches see people's needs and are in a unique position to address the small arms epidemic, identifying its material, moral, ethical and spiritual dimensions.

CCIA Policy Framework and Guidelines on Small Arms and Light Weapons

submissions to the UN on issues of civil, religious and political rights in relation to specific country situations, or the situation of Indigenous peoples, minorities, refugees and internally displaced persons. Ecumenical partners gain access to the proceedings through the WCC's consultative status with the UN, and delegates from critical human-rights situations such as those in Nigeria, Colombia, Guatemala, Indonesia and other regions are invited to provide oral testimonies.

Recent efforts have been made to review and assess the work being done by the human-rights staff of specialized agencies, regional ecumenical organizations and representatives of churches to develop plans and strategies for common advocacy in the future.

Several consultations in Africa and Asia, organized in cooperation with regional ecumenical organizations, have encouraged training in dealing with religious violence and human-rights abuses, defending human rights, developing community-based prevention models, and establishing early-warning systems to defuse conflicts and violence.

Disarmament

The WCC advocates for the effective control and reduction of conventional weapons, in particular small arms and light weapons, the elimination of nuclear weapons and non-military approaches to peace and human security.

Following the Harare assembly, the WCC helped to form an International Action Network on Small Arms (IANSA). IANSA's membership of more than two hundred NGOs makes it one of the largest international NGO campaign networks since the anti-landmines campaign. Several ecumenical strategy consultations in Europe, Latin America and Africa helped to develop regional plans in combating small arms as well as

138

An ACT-financed demining team searches a school ground in Izniq that was used as a Serbian army base during the conflict in Kosovo.

coordinate efforts for churches' participation in this new global initiative. The WCC created the Ecumenical Network on Small Arms (ENSA) to facilitate sharing of information and coordinate advocacy among churches. An ecumenical team of experts participated in the UN Conference on the Illicit Trade in Small Arms and Light Weapons in All its Aspects, held in New York in July 2001. The Commission of the Churches on International Affairs in May 2001 adopted a policy framework and guidelines on small arms and light weapons.

The concern about nuclear weapons was the subject of a number of initiatives particularly aimed at the NATO states. In 1999, a WCC statement endorsed an appeal from churches in the NATO countries urging the alliance, then celebrating its fiftieth anniversary, to take action to eliminate nuclear weapons and, as steps towards this goal, to reduce the alert status of its member states' nuclear weapons and renounce the first use of nuclear weapons. The WCC addressed a similar appeal to the other states which have nuclear weapons.

The WCC executive committee in February 2004 reiterated its "grave and ongoing concern that certain policies and practices of nuclear-weapon states undermine international progress towards nuclear disarmament".

Following release of the statement, a WCC delegation met with ministers and government officials of five non-nuclear NATO states as well as with the NATO headquarters to ask them to take a more pro-active role within the organization to fulfill nuclear disarmament obligations undertaken in the framework of the Nuclear Non-Proliferation Treaty. This initiative and the full policy of the WCC on nuclear weapons were presented again in visits with missions and in public events at the conference of the parties to the Treaty in May 2005.

139

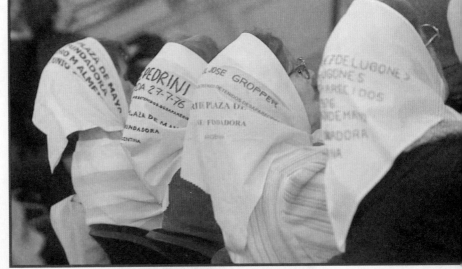

Argentine activists for peace and justice, member of Mothers of the Plaza de Mayo, attend a WCC presentation on globalization and violence.

Together with church representatives in the United States, in 2005 the CCIA began a dialogue with Muslims on nuclear weapons and disarmament. This is a way to explore an interfaith approach towards addressing the present complex role of nuclear arms in international relations and find a broad foundation for continued efforts towards reduction in numbers of these weapons.

Advocacy with the United Nations

In 1946, the Commission of the Churches on International Affairs was formed to ensure an effective relationship between the churches and the leadership of the new United Nations, and also to provide the main means to represent WCC member churches at the UN. The CCIA became one of the first international non-governmental organizations to be granted consultative status with the UN Economic and Social Council.

The WCC's UN office in New York monitors UN processes on priority issues for the WCC, conveys the WCC's concerns to appropriate UN bodies and government missions, coordinates actions with other church and NGO offices, and assists ecumenical delegations attending UN sessions.

Following an extensive evaluation process, in 2003 the WCC restructured its presence at the United Nations, both in New York and Geneva. A strategic task group on global advocacy, involving all WCC staff working on UN advocacy, has been formed to facilitate coordination, setting priorities and strategic planning. In November 2003, the WCC celebrated sixty years of Christian advocacy at the United Nations with an advocacy week in New York. The week increased the WCC's – and the churches' – visibility at the UN and allowed the WCC to identify new ways of working with churches worldwide in mutual shar-

140

ACT supports de-mining and land mine awareness efforts in Angola, where an estimated 86,000 people suffer from injuries sustained by land mine explosions.

ing and common strategizing on advocacy. The advocacy week has since become an annual event, bringing together about eighty key people responsible for international affairs and/or advocacy issues in member churches and partners from all parts of the world.

The activities described in this chapter are the primary responsibility of the International Affairs, Peace and Human Security staff team.

George Togba of Liberia crafts metal crosses from cartridge shells left following his country's civil war.

Ecumenical Accompaniment Programme in Palestine and Israel

The worsening situation in Israel and the Occupied Palestinian Territories in 2001 demanded that churches match their strongly worded statements with action. Responding to an appeal to the WCC by the heads of churches and Christian communities in Jerusalem for presence and solidarity – an appeal supported by member churches and specialized ministries – the WCC executive committee in September

2001 recommended the development of an accompaniment programme.

Intensive efforts were made so that the Ecumenical Accompaniment Programme in Palestine and Israel (EAPPI) could begin on the ground as soon as possible. A common international training package and application and screening procedures were developed, a local coordination office set up, and funds pursued to ensure the viability of the programme. The first official group of ecumenical accompaniers (EAs) arrived in

A Palestinian demonstrator against the Israeli separation barrier carries a young olive tree symbolic of groves being destroyed.

141

"There was a time when we thought ours was the last struggle for liberty. Suddenly, one is struck by what is happening here. If one can help to make a difference or can be a friend in solidarity, it will be a step for the good of mankind."

Bishop Lunga ka Siboto, *Ethiopian Episcopal Church, second vice president of the South African Council of Churches, as he began service as an ecumenical accompanier in September 2004*

August 2002. By June 2005, 198 accompaniers from more than thirty churches and ecumenical partners in 13 countries had served in the West Bank, Gaza Strip and Israel. EAs have come from Canada, Denmark, France, Germany, Ireland, New Zealand, Norway, South Africa, Sweden, Switzerland, the United Kingdom and the United States.

Most accompaniers stay for three months; some stay longer. Their task is to accompany Palestinians and Israelis in their non-violent actions and concerted advocacy efforts to end the occupation. Accompaniers serve in a variety of placements. Some placements involve more active work, such as advocating for a gate to remain open, assisting a mobile health clinic, or doing art therapy sessions in a refugee camp. Others involve simply presence, such as living in a village that is under threat from settlers, accompanying Israeli peace activists at demonstrations and Palestinian children to school through checkpoints and settlement areas. In all cases, EAs are there to support the initiatives of the local churches and peace activists, and simply to be in solidarity with the local population.

Accompaniers are strongly encouraged to write and share their direct experiences, with stories and photos posted daily at www.eappi.org. Upon return to their home country they engage in

143

further awareness-raising and advocacy through presentations in their
parishes and congregations, interviews
and articles in the media, but also
meetings with local governments,
members of the European Union par-
liament and the US congress, in order
to change public opinion.

While it is a WCC project, the EAPPI is
first and foremost an ecumenical initiative that brings together churches
and church-related organizations in
Jerusalem with WCC member churches and WCC-related ecumenical
organizations who have asked to be
part of the EAPPI. The programme has
proved to be a concrete manifestation
of Christian witness for justice, peace
and reconciliation in the Middle East.

EAPPI website:
http://www.eappi.org

*Opposite: Rockets and
bulldozers of the Israeli
occupying forces have
scarred homes,
businesses and agencies
in Jenin on the West
Bank. Above: Mtanios
Haddad, archimandrite of
the Greek Catholic
(Melkite) church in
Jerusalem, greets Ann-
Catrin Andersson, an
EAPPI accompanier from
Sweden.*

Focus on Africa

Accompanying the peace process in Sudan and empowering the voices of local Christians in their future has been a powerful statement of international ecumenical solidarity in situations of long-standing conflict. Far from being recipients of aid, African churches have shared their hope, energy and inspiration with the rest of the ecumenical movement in addressing religious plurality, economic justice, violence and reconciliation.

We, African people on the continent and in the diaspora,
Having been reminded afresh of our difficult past.
But, inspired by the stories of resistance with courage and sacrifice of our
      foreparents,
And empowered by the signs of hope such as increasing acceptance of dem-
      ocratic governance, the end of the apartheid regime, and the Truth and
      Reconciliation Commission of South Africa,
We hereby renew our commitment to reconstruct and rebuild our communi-
      ties and work tirelessly for a future of Africa full of life in abundance.
From Our Covenant with God, Harare 1998

A youthful participant in the Africa plenary session at the eighth assembly of the WCC, Harare 1998.

In Harare, participants joined with the churches in Africa in a commitment to place a special focus on Africa at the beginning of the 21st century, encouraging churches to:

- continue working for just social, political and economic system and institutions;
- seek and pursue peace and reconciliation;
- work towards the establishment of appropriate ethical values in work, governance and management, good stewardship;
- help contain and overcome the scourge of HIV/AIDS;
- affirm the rights of African children to hope for a bright future.

The special focus on Africa was one of the top considerations by the executive committee meeting after Harare, and further support for ecumenical work in Africa was encouraged by the central committee in 1999 which called for an integrated approach by the WCC on the impact of war and conflict, economic justice, spirituality and ethical values.

Impact of war and efforts for peace

WCC general secretary Konrad Raiser modelled the ecumenical movement's solidarity particularly through his official visits to African countries. Such visits aim to express pastoral solidarity and ensure those in sometimes intensely tragic conflicts and circumstances that the international ecumenical movement is in prayer with them, and actively working to address the conditions in which they find themselves. Many times, the occasion of the visit by the WCC general secretary also helps national churches and councils to express and strengthen their

145

WCC general secretary Konrad Raiser walks with a welcoming party of 1,000 from a small airstrip to the centre of the village of Yirol in southern Sudan, July 2002.

As we pondered on the genocide stories, we were convinced that the perpetrators of the genocide killed their humanness, cut off their relationship with God, before they could take away the humanness of others. The depth of the horror challenged us to deeply reflect on ways and strategies with which we can build everlasting peace in Rwanda in particular and the rest of Africa in general... This is an experience that teaches us to struggle for peace at all costs... Many countries on our continent have the potential of repeating the Rwandan experience, and now that we have time to prevent a similar occurrence, we commit ourselves that never again should such a degree of violence and crime against humanity [be] allowed to occur in any of our countries.

Statement from "Lasting Peace in Africa",

Rwanda, 16-19 April 2004

advocacy and moral stance in political and civil society settings.

In 2000, a high-level delegation led by the WCC and the All Africa Conference of Churches (AACC) general secretaries went to the Democratic Republic of Congo. The situation in the Congo, and the Great Lakes region in general, has been an active concern for the WCC for over a decade in efforts to bring about a just and lasting peace in the region. In 1999, the WCC helped mobilize support for the Lusaka peace agreement. Continued efforts supported the churches' role in the peace process leading to the April 2003 Sun City agreement. Both agreements have been instrumental in restoring peace to the region, although much more work needs to be done towards a peaceful settlement, particularly between Congo and Rwanda.

Raiser visited Nigeria in 2001 and discussed introduction of Muslim law, *sharia*, in parts of the country, and the danger churches saw this bringing to religious freedom. He also visited Southern Africa to discuss church responses to HIV/AIDS and attempts to end conflict in the region, particularly the civil war in Angola. Raiser led a delegation to Angola in 2003 as that country struggles out of a long-term conflict.

In 2002, Raiser headed a delegation to the Greater Horn of Africa and to the International Tribunal for Rwanda in Arusha, Tanzania, that expressed solidarity with those in that war-torn area of Sudan, Ethiopia and Eritrea, and focused on root causes of conflict and violence there. Promoting dialogue and understanding between Christian and Muslim communities was found to be essential if long-term peace and justice are to be achieved.

A survivor of the Rwandan genocide tells of his experience on the tenth anniversary of the massacre, April 2005.

In 2004, WCC general secretary Samuel Kobia visited Rwanda at the occasion of the tenth anniversary of the genocide, and spoke at the conference on "Lasting Peace in Africa".

The WCC works on peace and reconciliation efforts in Africa at many levels. Ecumenical delegations visited a number of countries such as Sierre Leone, Côte d'Ivoire and Congo-Brazzaville to provide support to churches in peace processes and to assess how the international ecumenical movement can best respond. The WCC supported efforts of the Inter-Faith Council of Liberia and the Liberian Council of Churches before and during the peace negotiation in Accra, Ghana. It was in part because of their strong advocacy and lobbying work that the peace agreement was successfully signed in 2003. The Inter-Faith Council now actively monitors the implementation of the peace agreement by all the parties involved.

The deteriorating situation in Zimbabwe called for special accompaniment of the churches in the country, including supporting ecumenical election monitors in 2001, addressing regional and international economic issues as root causes of violence, and providing safe spaces for sharing and planning. A specific dialogue begun in 2003 with Zimbabwe churches and ecumenical partners using the Sudan Ecumenical Forum (SEF) as a model has allowed Zimbabwe churches and the wider ecumenical family to discuss the situation and actions to help resolve the conflicts in the country.

Contacts were established for the Somalia peace talks at the beginning of 2003. The WCC's accompaniment was warmly welcomed by the part-

147

A family that had been internally displaced during the Angolan civil war makes its way home to Sanza-Pombo in the northern province of Uige.

Above: Women in the village of Gangura in the Sudanese province of Western Equatoria.

ners involved; the moderator of WCC's Commission of the Churches on International Affairs, Bethuel Kiplagat, is the chair of the peace talks. In particular, the WCC made possible the participation of Somali women, who had been excluded, in the negotiations.

Women-to-women solidarity visits were made to Sierra Leone, Liberia, Angola, Rwanda and Burundi, and the Sudan, in cooperation with the AACC, the Lutheran World Federation and the World YWCA. The stories of women's suffering, resilience and participation in peace and reconciliation processes in Africa were told in vivid reports published by the WCC.

A June/July WCC-AACC women's solidarity visit to Sudan in 2004 was able to meet with women who do not normally get a chance to tell their stories – of violence, desperation, displacement.

The delegation went to a camp for internally displaced persons (IDPs). There are four million IDPs registered in Sudan, many of whom have not been settled for over ten years.

"From what Sudanese women said, it is clear that women play the most important role in post-war Sudan," the WCC delegation member said. *"Their husbands have either been killed in the war or are still in the war zone, so the women have had to look after the children and to be the bread-winners as well as the decision-makers of the family."*

The delegation was also reminded once again, through the fighting in the Darfur region, of how rape of women has been used as a systematic, intentional weapon of war. "Sexual violence has been used to suppress the will of the people as well as an instrument of ethnic cleansing."

The delegation also saw how the Sudan Council of Churches and women's organizations of member churches have initiated projects for economic self-sufficiency and peace, and for the care of children, particularly orphans and street children.

But in addition to all other devastating tragedies facing the people of this country, there is one more: "AIDS is present here and we are so afraid of it – more than the war that has displaced us from the South," said a woman who was forced to move to Medani, a four-hour trip from Khartoum. "AIDS is now the greatest battle we have to fight."

In Africa, and around the world, the proliferation of small arms and light weapons contributes to escalating and prolonging violence. As part of the effort to curb the trade in small arms and light weapons, the WCC, in cooperation with the Fellowship of Christian Councils and Churches in West Africa (FECCIWA), hosted a consultation on small arms in West Africa in 2002. Representatives and experts from twelve West African countries and a variety of concerned organizations were invited to attend and share their experiences and ideas. The churches and ecumenical organizations were able to develop a regional plan of action to tackle armed violence and the unlawful use of small arms throughout the region.

The WCC formed a Council-wide staff group, the Africa Peace Monitoring Group (APMG), which brought colleagues from different teams together to address the critical situations in Africa from programme and communication perspectives. Since then, most of the WCC responses are reviewed and contributed to from the APMG, allowing for a fuller, integrated approach.

The WCC, through statements by the central committee, the executive

Left: Angolan children in Luanda, displaced by the civil war, share scarce food. Right: A girl in Luena, Angola, accentuates the positive.

committee and letters from the general secretary, has also addressed critical areas and issues in Africa requiring concerted international advocacy, particularly Sudan and Zimbabwe.

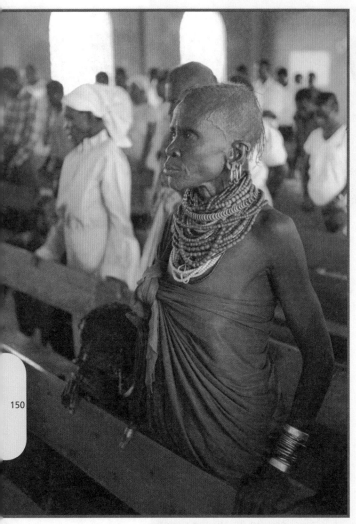

150

Sunday worship in the Africa Inland Church of Lokichokio, a village in the Turkana region of northern Kenya.

Accompanying peace processes in Sudan

A major concern at the Harare assembly was the conflict in Sudan, already then considered as Africa's longest-running civil war. Apart from an 11-year period of peace (1971-82), Sudan has been torn apart by civil war since its independence in 1956. The current conflict broke out in 1982 when the government tried to enforce Islamic *sharia* law in the country, triggering a rebellion beginning in the south, which is inhabited by African Christians and people belonging to traditional religions. The civil war in the Sudan has left some two million people dead and over four million displaced.

The peace protocols signed at the end of May 2004 raised hopes of an end to the war and the beginning of the long process of reconstruction and reconciliation. This agreement did not include the Darfur region in western Sudan, where tens of thousands were killed and over one mil-

lion displaced in 2004 alone, due to militia bands and in spite of demands by the international community that the Sudanese government protect its citizens.

The WCC has been active in peace-making efforts in the Sudan since the 1960s, and was instrumental in brokering the peace agreement in the early 1970s.

In recent peace-making efforts, the WCC supports the engagement of its ecumenical partners: the Sudan Council of Churches, the New Sudan Council of Churches, the Sudan Ecumenical Forum, the All Africa Conference of Churches and the National Council of Churches in Kenya.

In response to a request from the SEF, Samuel Kobia was named in 2003 as a special ecumenical envoy to monitor and contribute to the peace process. The appointment provided visible support and input from the churches to the Inter-Governmental Authority on Development (IGAD) peace process. The envoy played a discrete role of enabling dialogue between the conflicting parties, as a result of which the involved governments invited the WCC to be one of the international organizations to witness the planned peace agreement.

The WCC worked closely with the Catholic and Anglican churches in Sudan and other churches and ecumenical partners in the region. It

A class meets in the shade at the village school of Narus in southern Sudan.

upheld the potential role of the churches in the building of a new Sudanese society, in three broad areas: support for a process of peace, reconciliation and forgiveness; laying the foundation for a renewed civil society and democracy, including the reintegration of millions of combatants and displaced people; and contributing to the reconstruction of the devastated fabric of the country, especially in the areas of education and health care.

A Decade to Overcome Violence intern worked for two months as a liaison in Nairobi, connecting with church leaders involved in Sudan peace work, and highlighting the DOV. Grants provided further practical support to the councils of churches to help facilitate their efforts at peace and reconciliation, especially enabling young people and women in the grassroots movements to take part in the peace talks. A WCC-AACC women solidarity visit took place in July 2004.

Through Action by Churches Together (ACT) International, the WCC supported the international churches' humanitarian response to the Sudan crisis.

The crisis demands continued strong accompaniment by the international ecumenical fellowship. "The churches of the Sudan will face significant challenges after any peace accord," said an AACC staff member. "Forgiveness and reconciliation will be very important in a post-war Sudan, and the churches will have to lead the way."

Celebratory worship in Trinity cathedral at Addis Ababa, Ethiopia.

Economic justice

In placing a special focus on Africa, the Harare assembly spoke out regarding debt cancellation, the need for economic justice in order to address root causes of violence, instability, health crises and the need to work towards creating and supporting just and sustainable communities.

Over thirty African countries are categorized as "heavily indebted" – almost all in sub-Saharan Africa, also the hardest hit in the AIDS pandemic. The WCC pursued debt cancellation in the context of its economic globalization work.

In promoting dialogue between church, civil society and the state in Africa, support was given to the regional fellowships of councils and churches and to BEACON (Building Eastern African Community Network) to respond to the emerging economic and political initiatives in Africa. Several consultations in 2002 and 2003 dealt with the church response to NEPAD (New Partnership for Africa's Development), an initiative for economic emancipation spearheaded by some political leaders in Africa. Helping churches respond to NEPAD aims to ensure that the discussions around NEPAD did not remain a preserve of a small political elite but grow into a movement for all African people.

In 2001, work began to examine evidence of economic violence in Southern Africa through study of agrarian and land policies, to identify responses to this violence, and to make recommendations on how to deal with such violence within the broader framework of economic globalization.

Strengthening spirituality and ethical values

Peace, healing, reconciliation and justice are constant themes undergirding the churches' spiritual and practical mission in Africa. Subregional and continental meetings bring church and ecumenical participants to share experiences from their local and national situations and develop plans of action.

In early 2003, a major consultation on issues of peace, justice and human rights in Africa brought together sixty participants and mapped out a common framework for ecumenical action on the continent. Concurrently, a workshop on healing and reconciliation helped to facilitate the emergence of a network of African theologians concerned about justice, peace and reconciliation. It also provided the opportunity to renew a process of theological reflection on ecumenical thought and social concerns in the African continent in the context of globalization and violence.

The WCC, together with the AACC, regional fellowships and national councils, brought church leaders, including women and youth, to discuss the issue of corruption with the objective to develop a concrete plan of action. A working document, the "Charter for the Truth", was developed.

153

Priests and cantors celebrate the tenth anniversary of the enthronement of His Holiness Abuna Paulos, patriarch of Ethiopia. Addis Ababa, July 2002.

Efforts were made to collect and share more fully Africa's contribution to the life and work of the ecumenical movement. In a report published for the ninth assembly, "Ecumenical Social Responsibility and Democracy in Africa", material gathered from national councils of churches in Africa serves as a basis for putting together guidelines for churches' involvement in promoting and sustaining democracy and governance.

A dialogue process begun jointly by WCC and the Pontifical Council for Interreligious Dialogue "paid homage" to the contribution of African religious and spiritual vitality in Africa and all over the world through the diaspora. Three consultations (Nigeria 2001, Senegal 2002, Ethiopia 2004) reaf-

firmed "Africa's Contribution to the Religious and Spiritual Heritage of the World". Representatives came from Christian and Muslim communities in Africa, followers of African traditional religion as well as representatives of some of the various religious communities of Africa in the diaspora. The positive, uniting spirit of the consultations brought forth values they held in common, and African values that "the world needs to heed". A book has gathered contributions to date.

One of the most moving parts of the third consultation was the struggle of an Iraqi woman of African descent to join the meeting in Addis Ababa. Staff had learned about her through a Washington Post *article in early January 2004. Thawra Yousif* belongs to a community in Basra, whose existence is the legacy of slavery throughout the Middle East, one thousand years old. Arab traders brought Africans across the Indian Ocean from present-day Kenya, Tanzania, Sudan, Ethiopia and elsewhere in East Africa to Iraq, Iran, Kuwait, Turkey and other parts of the Middle East. Though centuries have passed since the first Africans, called Zanj, arrived in Iraq, some African traditions still persist. Thawra Yousif is a doctoral candidate in theatre and acting at Baghdad University's college of fine arts.

Finding Thawra Yousif was not easy. Hans von Sponeck, the former UN humanitarian coordinator for Iraq, went out of his way to locate her. Finally, after many months, staff received an e-mail. She would do anything to participate in the consultation. And she did. She tried to go from Basra to Kuwait and from there on a flight to Addis. The Kuwaiti authorities prevented her transit. She went the dangerous way to the Jordanian border and was turned back by the Jordanian border control. Then she tried via Damascus. And finally her persistence paid off.

As she entered the room, the participants in the consultation stood up and applauded her. Her presence, her stories about the Zanj in Iraq, how they sang and lived their daily trials, surviving through thinking of Africa, came to incarnate the very meaning of the consultation: Africa as the continent bringing together its

children from all over the world, people who have never forgotten Africa, who have always longed to go back, people who now together could celebrate being together.
Consultation on Africa's contribution to the religious and spiritual heritage of the world, Ethiopia 2004

Enabling and empowering the ecumenical movement in Africa

The assembly called for building the capacity of the churches and ecumenical movement in Africa to strengthen their moral and spiritual leadership and equip them to help build sustainable societies. The reconstructing Africa programme of dialogue and study was identified as an area that could be further developed, with an emphasis on capacity-building and information-sharing.

As a foundation for such work, the first joint meeting of WCC and AACC central committee members was held in Nairobi in 2001. The meeting was an opportunity for participants to discuss what it meant for both organizations to share in the one ecumenical movement and how each could maintain awareness of what the other was doing. Follow-up meetings for sub-regions of Africa were held later in the year.

Training and capacity-building strengthened ecumenical efforts in Africa and other regions. Six ecumenical enablers were identified, and they offer support across the continent to churches and ecumenical

AIDS!
**Stigma kills I care...do you?
The churches say YES!**

156

An adult entry from Sudan in the EAA poster competition opposing stigma and discrimination. Artist: Rabiel Poulino Loggali

out all of Africa. A vision process was engaged and provided direct guidance for the AACC general assembly in November 2003 and enabled a smooth leadership transition when Bishop Mvume Dandala became general secretary.

Nearly one hundred church educators and ecumenical leaders from 25 countries in Africa met in Johannesburg in September 2002 at a ground-breaking conference, "Journey of Hope in Africa Continued". The conference evaluated theological education and ecumenical formation with the aim of developing new ecumenical leadership for the continent. New methodologies of teaching theology within the African theological institutions, they said, should deal with social, political, economic, ethnic and gender issues, as well as conflict resolution and management, HIV/AIDS and other opportunistic diseases (cf. Ecumenical HIV/AIDS Initiative in Africa p. 67).

The WCC sponsored a group of African journalists in 2002 to come to the WCC to learn more about the international ecumenical movement's response to issues of concern to Africa, and also to give feedback on how the WCC could be more effective in reaching African media.

bodies on behalf of the WCC in leadership and management training, ecumenical formation, round-table facilitation and strategic planning.

During a critical transition period for the All Africa Conference of Churches, the WCC seconded one of its staff to serve as interim general secretary of the AACC. This had an immensely positive effect on the staff of the AACC as well as its partners. Through the appointment, the AACC was assured of the worldwide ecumenical commitment to Africa, which inspired renewed confidence in and commitment to the AACC through-

An integrated effort

The focus on Africa was integrated into activities throughout the Council. Thus peace and reconciliation work called on those with programme responsibilities in international affairs, regional relations, church and ecumenical relations, public information, education, interreligious relations, economic justice, women, youth and more – all were involved in identifying needs and working with partners regionally and internationally, to bring the whole of the ecumenical movement to bear in the task of building just and sustainable communities in Africa.

157

An adult entry from Sudan in the EAA poster competition promoting the churches' ministries to people living with HIV/AIDS. Artist: David Daniel

Communicating
the Ecumenical Story

Use of new communication technologies means more people have access to WCC information and can be involved in the international ecumenical movement, supported by expanded services for media, new publications and improved distribution networks.

The WCC has a story to tell – of unity, transformation, struggle and hope. Such stories have been told throughout this report. The strategies and tools that help to tell these stories continue to be refined to meet changing events, resources, technological possibilities and needs.

The eighth assembly was the first WCC assembly reported using the possibilities of the internet, allowing thousands of people not present in Harare to follow the business and events of the gathering.

At its first meeting following the assembly, the central committee reviewed communication strategies in response to the programme guidelines committee's call for clear implementation of an integrated communication strategy and process throughout the WCC. The strategies paper set out management priorities, objectives and principles to be used as a basis for communicating the work of the WCC.

The central committee emphasized that communication is fundamental

UN secretary general Kofi Anan (third from left) and representatives of several faiths at the St Pierre cathedral service for the "Geneva 2000" social summit, June 2000.

to all aspects of the work of the WCC. It is a process which starts in the initial phases of shaping programmes – not simply a matter of getting messages out once a programme or initiative is under way. The committee affirmed ways to express the fellowship through empowering local communities and communicators to share their experiences of ecumenism, and to tell stories appropriate to each region. And in keeping with decisions made in Harare, they encouraged a focus on Africa in the WCC's communication.

Certainly some of the WCC's best efforts have been when programme and communication work together on clearly defined priorities and events – planning together, committing time and appropriate funding. Events such as the World Conference on Racism, Geneva 2000, the Faith and Order Plenary Commission at Kuala Lumpur in 2004, the World Day of Prayer for Peace launched in 2004 and the CWME conference in Athens in 2005 have used multiple communication formats – including publications, web, press work, video, photography, seconded journalists and more. Much of the work is done in four or more languages.

The WCC has always wrestled with the best way to communicate its activities – and not only in format and language. Some activities dealing with sensitive issues are intentionally given a low profile in order to protect the space for dialogue. Many of the programmes, which deal with long-term processes and progress, are hard to "sell" to journalists looking for action and results. Channelling sufficient human and financial resources into selected high-profile events has been both desired in terms of visibility and viewed with trepidation because of the resources and attention drawn away from vital long-standing work in which the ecumenical movement is engaged. And the reality of a worldwide fellowship means seeking new ways to make connections and share information

159

Beauty Maenzanise, a United Methodist from Zimbabwe, participates in the ecumenical team promoting "a change of heart" during an NGO gathering at Geneva 2000.

across cultures, traditions, interests, access and languages.

Enhancing communication strategies, skills and networks

The WCC develops and implements strategic communication efforts to *highlight issues* and events such as the launch of the Decade to Overcome Violence, economic global-ization, for example Geneva 2000, and the high-level encounters with the Bretton Woods institutions, as well as international church response to the Iraq war. Other efforts ensure that priority events, such as the elec-tion of the new WCC general secre-tary in 2003 and the reconfiguration of the ecumenical movement discus-sion, the world mission conference and the assembly of the WCC are appropriately communicated to the

WCC constituency, media and the general public.

Communication sessions at central committee meetings were begun to assist members to be better commu-nicators about the WCC in their own constituencies. Such direct communi-cation – where experience and per-sonal perspective give a sense of life and relevance to the WCC – is in many cases the most effective way to communicate the fundamental pur-pose and work of the Council.

The WCC supported the renewal of the global communicators' network for communicators working in and for churches and church-related organizations. Beginning in 2004, the WCC along with the Lutheran World Federation took on coordina-tion of the network.

Raising the voice of the churches through the media

The core elements of WCC communication have long been: identifying WCC issues and events of interest to church and secular media; writing and distributing press releases, updates, features and other targeted material in four languages; and responding to media inquiries. Following the Harare assembly, the WCC expanded its output for secular and religious media in terms of format, content and languages.

Intensive efforts have been made to improve relationships with media — working with media to respond to their interests and improve their knowledge of ecumenical issues, and expanding the WCC's understanding of how best to work with media. Carefully targeted distribution of press material in terms of language, format and subject has continued to be improved.

Efforts in media relations have sought to build the credibility and visibility of the WCC by highlighting the expertise and the alternative perspective provided by the WCC on issues and events reported in the mainstream media.

Coverage of official visits and meetings includes working cooperatively as much as possible with other church and ecumenical communicators, especially in initiating local coverage of events outside Geneva.

Intensive press operations are also set up at major WCC meetings, such

161

Opposite: Balai Latihan Pendiokan vocational training centre near Tomohon, North Sulawesi, Indonesia. Right: Konrad Raiser is interviewed after meeting with Ethiopian president Girma W. Giorgis, Addis Ababa, 2002.

as central committee meetings, the Faith and Order Commission plenary, and the conference on world mission and evangelism. Preparations for the WCC assembly in Porto Alegre in 2006 have meant new efforts to network and promote the WCC, including communication in Portuguese.

Working together to communicate "fellowship"

Ecumenical issues and the often complex work of the WCC are best communicated when journalists, media representatives and WCC communicators actually work together in researching and experiencing common projects. This active involvement of communicators has helped the WCC to engage in a critical exchange on ecumenical issues, bringing new perspectives and challenges.

One such event was an "exposure visit" to Geneva for journalists from Africa in September 2001, which resulted in improved understanding

"We've always thought of you as an important advocate for refugees on the global level, but did not realize the depth of your commitment to Africa. We see you differently now."

US mission staff member *on learning WCC brought journalists from Africa to cover a UN High Commissioner for Refugees meeting with non-governmental organizations*

and coverage of WCC events, particularly on issues of uprooted people. The visit served to expand contacts with journalists in the sub-regions. An additional benefit was that the visit raised the WCC profile at the United Nations High Commissioner for Refugees.

A resident journalist programme was developed which offered the opportunity for a journalist to spend a significant amount of time at the WCC offices in Geneva and to write about key ecumenical issues for his or her constituency. Funding was found to sponsor two journalists – a print journalist from Mozambique in 2000 and an independent Orthodox video producer from Bulgaria who followed the WCC's course on lay leadership training in the Middle East in 2002.

To cite another example, an intern from Zimbabwe served with the WCC for one year as a "communication officer for Africa". He established a database for better networking with

African ecumenical leaders and communicators, improved internal communication with the Africa task force and Africa peace monitoring group, and strengthened understanding of communication issues in Africa.

The WCC sponsors a small number of journalists who come to Geneva to attend and cover the WCC central committee meetings. The journalists are selected through applications to represent different languages, regions and media. The opportunity was designed to expose journalists to the work of the WCC and the ecumenical movement, expand print and radio coverage of central committee issues and events, enhancing relationships with communication networks in different regions.

WCC News, a concise newsletter covering WCC activities and issues, was first issued in December 1999 in four languages. The initial practice was to bring in guest editors from churches and ecumenical organizations to help

them better understand the work of the WCC and ecumenism, make links and allow an exchange between them and WCC communication staff on communication challenges in their contexts. After budget restrictions at the end of 2002, the guest editor programme could no longer be funded, but the reach of the newsletter was expanded through electronic as well as print distribution.

Building electronic platforms for information-sharing

From being the first official church institution to have a page on the World Wide Web – launched on 14 February 1994 – the WCC's web presence has grown to include multiple, targeted sites reaching a vast public.

At the end of 2003, the WCC websites contained over 7000 pages, most of them in the four working languages of the WCC (English, German, French and Spanish) with a

Left: NGOs demonstrate at the Geneva 2000 social summit. Centre: Mauricio Andrade of Brazil's Episcopal Anglican church is interviewed at the World Social Forum, Porto Alegre, 2003. Right: Street scene in a time of turmoil, Port-au-Prince, Haiti, February 2004.

163

Sunday worship in the Presbyterian church in Imere, on the outskirts of Port Vila, Vanuatu.

number of pages also available in Russian. That year, the websites had almost six million hits – single requests. Since the year 2000, the number of hits has almost doubled every year, making it the single most utilized channel of communication.

The website has become the most comprehensive source of information about the WCC and shows most clearly how the work and efforts of the WCC are integrated across programmes and issues.
In addition to the WCC's main site, special websites have been developed for key activities and audiences, such as the Decade to Overcome Violence, the Ecumenical Accompaniment Programme in Palestine and Israel (EAPPI), and youth.

A new information-sharing web platform, *Ecuspace.net*, was also developed to enhance cooperative information-sharing and dialogue among partners. The site allows for different access levels for discussion among specific groups and sharing of draft documents. (See also "Stabilizing funding and seeking new sources of support", p.172)

In the last several years, new technology has been used to provide "on-line services" allowing interested individuals to sign up to receive press information, newsletters and programme updates via e-mail. Such service is both cost-effective and enables a larger public to be more informed about ecumenical issues and WCC events.

Providing visual images of church and ecumenical life

The WCC has been considered a primary resource for visual images of global Christian life through *PhotoOikomene*, which provides professional photographs and video footage illustrating the issues and events important in the ecumenical movement. The on-line service was enhanced through a new website launched in summer 2003, which has made thousands of WCC photos available through a searchable database.

Video production, which had to be curtailed beginning in 2003 due to financial cuts, included several award-winning productions such as *Facing the Future*, an educational DVD containing seven videos targeting youth and young adults aged 15-28, and *The Roots of Violence*, a prize-winning video about peace, reconciliation and faith in Sierra Leone produced in cooperation with the Ecumenical Council in Denmark and Danish TV1.

Various exhibitions, including a new mobile WCC exhibit, were designed and produced. An updated WCC logo was commissioned, to bring new life and movement to the oikoumene symbol for the 21st century.

Telling the ecumenical story through books and other diverse media

WCC publications have been considered by many as the mainstay of communication of ecumenical reflection and issues. The post-Harare period was overshadowed by the sudden death of Marlin VanElderen, executive editor of WCC publications, in 2000 and the death of Jan Kok, coordinator of publications and documentation, in 2002. Their combined 47 years of service to communicating ecumenism and the WCC has left a legacy of wisdom, passion and commitment to telling the ecumenical story. Their sudden absence resulted in what one colleague characterized

as "wilderness wandering" until publications staff could regroup and reorient themselves.

During the period between assemblies, several significant books were published; special mention may be given to the second edition of the *Dictionary of the Ecumenical Movement*, the third volume in the series *A History of the Ecumenical Movement* (1968-2000) and the second volume of *Growth in Agreement*, a compilation of reports on world bilateral dialogues. The 22-year-old ecumenical best-seller *Baptism, Eucharist and Ministry* achieved its 37th English-language printing in mid-2004. The annual WCC *Yearbook*, the quarterly journal *The Ecumenical Review* and the popular Risk book series were staples of an output that has been significantly influenced by such major themes identified in Harare as HIV/AIDS, Africa, overcoming violence, economic globalization and relations among the Orthodox, Protestants and Catholics. *The Ecumenical Review* and the *International Review of Mission* were both redesigned in 2004.

Major efforts and new initiatives have been undertaken to improve the distribution and to coordinate the production of WCC printed materials. Agreements with new distributors in the US, Canada and the UK, among others, help to ensure better publicity and access to major markets, including increased distribution of WCC publications in university and theological libraries and book-shops. The development of on-line sales and distribution through the WCC website has also improved access to WCC publications. Copyright requests to use worship materials and other resources arrive daily. A WCC bookshop serves staff and visitors to the Ecumenical Centre in Geneva.

New emphases on collaboration and co-productions with other publishers have enabled more publications in languages such as French, German, Italian, Greek, Russian, Spanish and Portuguese. WCC publications are promoted, and relationships with other publishers enhanced, through participation at international book fairs and academic events such as the Frankfurt book fair and the American Academy of Religion annual conference in the USA.

Preserving ecumenical memory and providing visions for the future

On the occasion of its 200th anniversary the Banque Pictet, a Geneva bank, made a major donation to the WCC in 2003 for the creation of a "world centre of excellence for ecumenical research".

This research centre, which was completed in mid-2005, has been located on two sites. The library and archives building at the Ecumenical Centre in Geneva now houses the historical book collection (prior to 1968) and electronic, audio, visual and paper archives of the ecumenical movement. Thanks to the grant, thousands of WCC resources have been preserved and archived, and are now accessible through a comprehensive database available worldwide.

166

A researcher in the library of the Ecumenical Centre, Geneva.

A redeveloped library facility at the Ecumenical Institute at the Château de Bossey houses the modern library collection of books and resources which serves the "ecumenical laboratory" that is centred at the Ecumenical Institute.

Supporting a multi-lingual ecumenical movement

Communicating in multiple languages – most particularly English, French, Spanish and German – has been essential in maintaining and strengthening a worldwide fellowship. The WCC translates many of its working documents and resources into its working languages, in addition to commissioning occasional translations into and out of Arabic, Russian, Greek and Portuguese. Interpretation for major WCC meetings, and in response to individual needs, is also arranged.

The WCC has also been working on a terminology project that will help others around the world to translate ecumenical material in multiple languages consistently and coherently.

All of these instruments, technologies, processes and skills help the WCC as a whole communicate its work and vision with a global audience.

The activities described in this chapter are the primary responsibility of two staff teams, Public Information, and Publications and Research.

Despite experiences reminiscent of Babel, interpreters of the ecumenical story delight in encountering the spirit of Pentecost.

167

Ecumenical News International (ENI)

ENI, a global news service reporting on ecumenical developments and other news of the churches, marked its tenth anniversary in 2004. ENI was launched in September 1994 as a cooperative venture by the World Council of Churches, the Lutheran World Federation, the World Alliance of Reformed Churches and the Conference of European Churches. ENI became a legally independent organization in January 2001, although from the beginning it was established as an independent, professional, ecumenical news agency.

ENI currently works with more than thirty part-time correspondents around the globe in addition to a core staff in Geneva. Its news stories are sent daily by e-mail to mass media, church newspapers libraries and church leaders and are regularly translated and published in over fifty countries.

The WCC remains the largest funder of ENI. An evaluation of ENI commissioned by the WCC in January 2001 affirmed the need for the news service that ENI provides on behalf of the ecumenical family. In 2004, the WCC executive committee reiterated its support for the original purpose of ENI and encouraged efforts that would allow ENI to achieve a more sustainable funding situation, including possible new alliances with other church-related news agencies.

ENI website: *http://www.eni.ch/*

Finance and Structure

Like so many organizations – secular and religious – the WCC has faced significant financial challenges and related structural changes over this period. But with careful control of expenses, active efforts to halt declines in income, and new initiatives to raise additional income, the WCC looks forward to a more positive financial future.

Implementing the ecumenical vision requires structure, management and a firm financial foundation, and the WCC and its governing bodies have constantly ensured responsible stewardship of human and financial resources to accompany and support the development of programme.

Yet the ecumenical vision and related needs have always exceeded its financial realities. The competition for resources and the current economic climate have only made this more true since Harare. Such realities have necessitated hard decisions about programme priorities and staffing. Yet they also have given new impetus to developing new and creative ways of working together.

Ensuring responsible stewardship through difficult times

After an overall surplus of 5.3 million Swiss francs in 1999 due to strong investment income, the WCC suffered an operating deficit of 750,000 Swiss francs in 2000 largely due to the poor performance of the

Council's investment portfolio. The difficult times continued through 2001 and 2002.

The central committee then called for an increase to general reserves of 1 million Swiss francs for 2003, to be achieved following an extensive adjustment of programmes and staffing. The programme adjustment promoted new ways of working. Some activities are carried out in closer collaboration with member churches and REOs. Examples are climate change, EDAN and the Indigenous peoples programmes. Two regional desks were relocated to the regions.

In August 2003 the central committee approved a funds and reserves policy which called for transparency in two broad areas. Firstly, funds are to be categorized into either unrestricted and designated funds or restricted funds to permit a clear picture of funds at the disposition of the Council, in distinction to those managed in accordance with the restrictions agreed with the Council's partners.

Second, the policy defined general reserves as those funds available to the Council after meeting its obligations and without recourse to its land, buildings and other fixed assets.

Financial results for 2003 reported a net surplus of 1.4 million Swiss francs. The general reserves, represented in liquid assets, totalled 1.8 million Swiss francs at that date and were increased to 3.4 million Swiss francs at 31 December 2004. The approved budget for 2005 anticipates an increase of 1.3 million Swiss francs to general reserves, to attain a total of 4.7 million Swiss francs at the end of 2005.

In August 2003, the central committee also issued a statement of investment objectives and policy, affirming the ethical guidelines governing the Council's investments. In addition, capital preservation was confirmed as the primary investment objective for the

Council's general investment funds, thus limiting future investment risk.

Membership contributions

The Harare assembly affirmed the principle that membership contributions should reach the goal of 10 million Swiss francs in five years – and charged that the churches must deepen their commitment and "wherever possible" exceed the minimum contribution. These undesignated funds from membership contributions are especially important because they provide substantial funding for the few core programmes that are not fully supported by major funding partners.

The membership campaign beginning after the Harare assembly set as a goal that all member churches should begin to pay their annual membership contribution by 2005. The central committee set the minimum membership contribution in

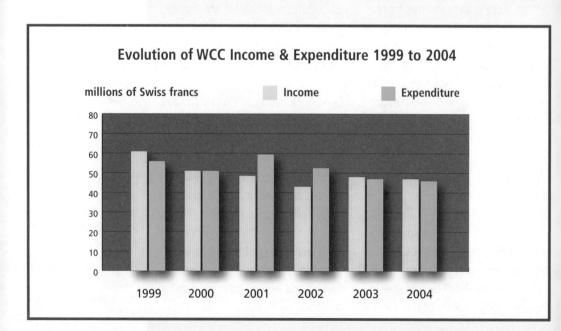

Evolution of WCC Income & Expenditure 1999 to 2004

millions of Swiss francs — Income — Expenditure

1999 2000 2001 2002 2003 2004

1998 at 1000 Swiss francs per year per church. The central committee also recognized that for some churches in the most impoverished areas of the world, alternative ways of making a contribution might need to be found.

A policy proposal reviewed by the executive committee in February 2003, and approved by the central committee later that year, asserted the principle that membership contributions – which are essential for the core functioning of the WCC – are to be considered compulsory, with non-payment leading to the loss of membership benefits.

Such benefits would include eligibility to receive subsidies for representatives or delegates to attend meetings of WCC governing bodies, committees and the assembly and other WCC meetings or events. In cases where churches have not paid any contribution over several years, they would be listed as non-active member churches, which implies that they are not eligible to send representatives or delegates to meetings of WCC governing bodies, committees and the assembly, and could not receive subsidies for other WCC meetings or events.

Through the membership campaign, more churches are now contributing. In 1998, 172 churches had paid a contribution. By 2002, 226 churches, out of a total membership of 342, had contributed 6.5 million Swiss francs to the WCC. In 2003 the num-

ber grew to 244 but dropped to 224 in 2004. In spite of the increase in the number of contributing member churches, the income over those years has remained virtually stable. However, with the decline in other forms of contribution, the membership income has become even more significant and now accounts for about 16 percent of the total budget.

In addition to clarifying principles around membership, the central committee also approved a new formula for calculating membership contribution, which aimed for a method that is "fair, transparent and objectively determined for all members".

The new membership contribution calculation is based on the size of the church, and the gross domestic product (GDP) of the country (or countries) where it is located. In specific cases where church members' income is significantly lower than the national average, the church can request an adjustment, to be authorized by the finance committee.

Churches that currently contribute more than the figure calculated in the new system are requested to maintain their level of contribution.

The new system was introduced as from 1 January 2004, with the first year seen as a transition period. Even so, initial results show a slight increase in membership contributions over 2003 figures. It is too early to assess the impact of the new system, especially for those churches "assessed" with a higher contribution amount than that paid in 2003.

Stabilizing funding and seeking new sources of support

Stabilizing current funding and seeking funds from "non-traditional" sources had become imperative objectives even before 2002.

The annual WCC round table has been steadily developed following its first meeting in 2000. It brings together representatives of partner organizations which together contribute over 80 percent of the funds for the WCC. The WCC presents programmes and priorities, and each organization present looks at their goals and discusses how to strengthen cooperation among various sectors of the ecumenical community. This annual encounter has become an increasingly useful tool of dialogue and collaboration at global level between churches, specialized ministries and the WCC.

The WCC also worked at ways to raise its profile through steady, professional effort as well as high-profile events such as visits by heads of state and high-level consultations.

New technologies have also helped strengthen the relationship with funding partners. The website, *ecuspace.net*, facilitates the "ecumenical partner's survey" where all members of the WCC round table provide information about their organization such as source of income, type of

programme priorities, or geographic presence. Data has been collected for the years 2000, 2001, 2002 and 2003. Each year this information is compiled and made available to all partners and generates stimulating debates on how to develop collaboration. The *ecuspace.net* is also used as a protected repository where partners can obtain planning and reporting documents from the WCC.

Efforts to raise funds from "non-traditional donors" have not so far yielded significant fruit, but there are promising signs in noting the specific types of projects that have been funded, such as HIV/AIDS, and the ecumenical research centre.

Financial challenges and the desire to find new ways of working together have also resulted in increased cooperation with member churches and partner organizations through seconded staff, collaboration on programme, and contribution of in-kind resources towards activities. Such concrete expressions of the fellowship of churches have strengthened bonds between churches and organizations. On behalf of the whole of the ecumenical movement, we owe a debt of gratitude to all churches and organizations that have been able to assist in this way.

The activities described in this chapter come from the following staff teams: General Secretariat; Human Resources; Finance; Income Monitoring and Development.

The Ecumenical Centre in Geneva: a Living and Welcoming Space

The Ecumenical Centre is home to an international and multicultural community of people drawn from many nations and many Christian traditions: a place to worship, a place to work, a place of encounters. Countless meetings are organized or hosted in this location. But the place is much more than a building for offices and meeting places. It is truly an "ecumenical space" where the living reality of the ecumenical fellowship and the multiplicity of its relationships may be experienced. Thousands of visitors are welcomed every year, ranging from groups of young people, Indigenous peoples to church leaders and political figures from all over the world.

The Centre was built in 1964 and is situated with views over Switzerland's national borders to the mountains in neighbouring France, a physical reminder of the ecumenical task of crossing borders between peoples and confessions. The Centre's chapel, library, rooms and grounds are shared with other bodies, including the Lutheran World Federation, the World Alliance of Reformed Churches, the Conference of

The service of installation of the Rev. Dr Samuel Kobia as WCC general secretary, in the chapel of the Ecumenical Centre, Geneva, February 2004.

European Churches, the World Student Christian Federation, as well as ACT International, ECLOF, Ecumenical News International, the Ecumenical Advocacy Alliance and representatives of the Ecumenical Patriarchate and Moscow Patriarchate. Some offices of UNAIDS and WHO-related organizations are also located at the Ecumenical Centre.

One of the features of the Ecumenical Centre chapel is that, despite generous use of stained glass from Denmark, wood from Ghana and icons given by Orthodox churches, the architect designed the space so that, no matter where one sits, one faces at least one pane of clear glass. Within the chapel, one is aware of the world around. Within the "Centre", one is reminded that one sits at the periphery of Creation. Those who engage in common prayer and meditation will be called once more to join the fellowship of far-flung churches and the life of the world God loves.

Towards a Common Understanding and Vision of the World Council of Churches

This commentary of the Common Understanding and Vision (CUV) document was published by the World Council of Churches in 1998. The full text is available from WCC Publications or on the Internet, http://wcc-coe.org/wcc/who/cuv-e.html

"Towards a Common Understanding and Vision of the World Council of Churches" is the title of a statement adopted by the central committee of the World Council of Churches in September 1997. It grew out of a study begun in 1989, and draws on insights from many churches, organizations, groups and individuals. The full text of this statement weaves together understandings that have emerged from fifty years of discussions within the WCC of the unity of the church with an overview and analysis of the contemporary challenges facing churches around the world in their life and witness and in their relations with one another. The eight affirmations [in this brochure] highlight some key features of the understanding of the World Council of Churches developed in that statement.

1. The World Council of Churches is a fellowship of churches which have committed themselves to make visible their unity in Christ and to call one another to a deeper expression of that unity through worship and common life, witness and service to the world.

The constitutional basis of the World Council of Churches says that the WCC is a "fellowship of churches". The word "fellowship" is a reminder that the WCC is not a body which acts separately from the churches. Nor is it a merely functional association set up to organize common activities.

In identifying themselves with the fellowship of the World Council, churches are acknowledging that the membership of the church of Christ is wider and more inclusive than the membership of their own church. Their quest for visible Christian unity is not a search for uniformity. The churches' fellowship in the WCC is not intended to create some kind of "super-church" into which all churches would dissolve and lose their identity.

Quite the contrary. The very diversity of the member churches enriches their fellowship in the Council. They come from all parts of the world. Their members speak many different languages. How they worship God and teach the Christian faith varies according to their historic traditions and their contemporary contexts.

All these churches - in the words of the WCC basis – "confess the Lord Jesus Christ as God and Saviour according to the scriptures". They seek fellowship with one another because, as the first assembly of the WCC said in 1948, "Christ has made us his own, and Christ is not divided".

This fellowship is not an end in itself. It exists in order to point to God's mission and activity in the world. The fellowship the churches have found in the World Council of Churches is not yet complete. But the WCC provides a space where they can explore what it means to be in fellowship towards greater unity and can challenge one another to manifest that unity more deeply.

Churches which participate in the Council open themselves to such challenges. They acknowledge that they are accountable to one another.

2. There have been many signs of growth towards Christian unity during the fifty years since the founding of the World Council of Churches.
During the past half-century the number of WCC member churches has more than doubled. At the same time, the Council has become much more truly a world body. Very nearly two-thirds of the original member churches came from Europe and North America. Today, nearly two-thirds are from the other parts of the globe.

Churches of almost every Christian tradition are involved in this movement towards the unity of the church. The Roman Catholic Church, though it is not a member of the WCC, maintains regular working relations with the Council.

The participation of women in the life of the WCC has increased; and their voices have been strengthened in ecumenical gatherings.

Signs of growth towards Christian unity can also be seen in what the churches have done together within the fellowship of the WCC.
They have offered assistance to those driven from their homes by war, violence, poverty and environmental destruction. They have expressed solidarity in prayer and encouragement with persecuted churches and churches seeking God's will in the midst of crisis.

Through the WCC churches have encouraged one another to witness together to Jesus Christ in places where the voice of only one church would not be heard. They have learned from one another's insights into questions of doctrine and life on which they are divided.

They have accepted the judgment that every form of racism, also in their own life, is contrary to the word and will of God. They have challenged each other to replace old bonds of dominance and dependence by new forms of partnership. They have worshipped together using each other's words and music, and they have learned to read the Bible through each other's eyes.

Over these fifty years, a growing number of new councils of churches and other local, national, regional and global bodies have come to share with the WCC in this task of working for the unity of the church.

3. It is impossible to speak about the World Council of Churches apart from the ecumenical movement, out of which it grew and of which it is an important instrument.
The World Council of Churches was formed by the merger of two earlier movements for the unity of the church: the Faith and Order movement, which focused on issues of doctrine that have divided the churches, and the Life and Work movement, which promoted collaboration by the churches in social action.

Their decision to join together in a body whose membership would be made up of churches responded to an appeal for the formation of a "league of churches" sent in 1920 by the Ecumenical Patriarch of Constantinople "to all churches everywhere".

The International Missionary Council, representing an even earlier stream of work for Christian unity, formally merged with the WCC in 1961. Ten years later, the World Council of Christian Education, whose roots lay in the Sunday school movement of the 18th century, became part of the Council.

Much of the energy behind the impulses for Christian unity in the early 20th century came from movements of young people and students. The WCC shares the responsibility to build on the legacy of the ecumenical movement with all who seek to promote the unity of the church and to bring Christians together to participate in God's healing of creation:

- regional, national and local councils of churches;
- organizations of churches of a single family or tradition;
- organizations representing a particular ecumenical constituency or serving a particular purpose or ministry;
- less formally structured Christian communities and movements;
- churches which are not members of the WCC but accept the call to make visible the oneness of the church.

4. Today, no less than when the WCC was founded fifty years ago, the world and the churches face a time of crisis whose deepest dimensions are spiritual.
The world has seen many hopeful political and social changes over the past half-century. But these have

177

been accompanied by new threats to the welfare of humanity and creation.

Colonialism has practically disappeared, but many of the nations to emerge from former colonies are subject to new kinds of economic and political dependency.

The fear of a global nuclear holocaust has receded with the end of the cold war. Yet wars are still being fought, often within countries and along racial or ethnic lines.

Religious loyalites are used to foment hatred and violence and the lives of religious minorities are often precarious, even though encounter between people of different faiths has become common in many places and religious freedom is established by law nearly everywhere.

Many military regimes have been replaced by democratically elected civilian governments. But political institutions are seeing their credibility diminish as evidence mounts of their ineffectiveness and corruption.

Widespread awareness of threats to the global environment has not yet been matched by the will to make radical changes in life-style.

As modern means of transportation and instantaneous worldwide communication bring people all around the world closer together, economic, financial and media powers are creating a kind of global unity. But its price has been a growing fragmenta-

tion of societies and exclusion for more and more of the human family. The moral foundations of human community have become more fragile. In this situation the churches have not always acted according to their commitments and convictions. Against the background of the spiritual crises of today, the people of God are called to repentance, conversion and renewal.

Are they able to live out a distinct alternative to the kind of global unity which comes by way of dominance and exclusion? Can they demonstrate a convincing model of relationships based on solidarity and sharing, mutual accountability and empowerment?

5. The contemporary spiritual crises call the ecumenical movement and the World Council of Churches to reaffirm the vocation of being an impulse for renewal.

The ecumenical movement of the 20th century has sought to bridge the gap between the churches as they are and the true fellowship with the triune God and among one another which is their calling and God's gift.

Within the ecumenical movement the World Council of Churches has sought to integrate the vision of John 17:21 ("that they may all be one... so that the world may believe") with the vision of Ephesians 1:10 (God's "plan for the fullness of time, to gather up all things in Christ, things in heaven and things on earth").

This vision, rooted in the life of the Christian churches, means that the ecumenical movement is more than merely a concern for interchurch relationships.

The ecumenical vision looks for the renewal of the church and the world in the light of the gospel of God's kingdom. In the face of every threat to life, it proclaims the Christian hope of life for all, the healing of the human community and the wholeness of God's entire creation.

In seeking this renewal, the ecumenical movement promotes cooperation and sharing, common witness and common action by the churches and their members. In each place and in all places, it is concerned with the true being and life of the church as an inclusive community.

The ecumenical movement is wider than the organizational forms it has taken. It has found expression in a rich variety of networks and initiatives for renewal among lay people, especially women and young people.

6. As part of their fellowship in the World Council, the member churches acknowledge a common calling, which they seek to fulfill together.
By belonging to the WCC a church acknowledges its willingness to identify itself in a visible, sustained and organized way with the goals of the ecumenical movement and the search for deeper fellowship.

Member churches of the Council seek:

- to nurture the ability to pray, live, act and grow together in community, dealing with disagreements through theological discussion, prayer and dialogue;
- to take responsibility for one another in a spirit of common faithfulness to the gospel rather than of judgment and exclusion;
- to join in service that extends beyond their own boundaries and to link their own local contexts with the global reality;
- to recognize that they are part of a fellowship that has a voice of its own and thus to give serious consideration to what the Council says and does on behalf of that fellowship;
- to implement within their own life the agreements reached through joint theological study and reflection by the fellowship as a whole;
- to support one another in times of need and struggle and to celebrate each other's joys and hopes;
- to understand the mission of the church as a joint responsibility that is shared with others, not undertaken in competition with them;
- to enter into a fellowship of worship and prayer with other churches;
- to take a full part in the life and work of the WCC and its activities and to contribute to the resources the Council needs to carry these out.

All this is summarized in the member churches' recognition of their "common calling" – a dynamic understanding of the WCC as a fellowship of pilgrims moving towards the same goal.

7. To help the churches to fulfill together their common calling, the WCC must have an effective organizational structure.

The essence of the World Council of Churches is the growing fellowship of its member churches on the way to full communion in faith, life and witness. This fellowship takes organized form in order to enable it to be an instrument for the pilgrimage towards unity.

To serve the ecumenical movement the Council must be able to respond to new challenges brought by changing times, growing discernment of the ecumenical calling and new ecumenical partners.

The structure of the Council should reflect its identity as a fellowship of churches. It should do justice to the plurality of cultures and theological and spiritual traditions represented in its member churches.

The WCC should work in an integrated way on the full range of the common calling which the churches acknowledge. And it should make evident how all of its work is rooted in the hope that God's purposes will not fail.

The Council has a unique identity as the most comprehensive and representative body among the many organized expressions of the ecumenical movement. This equips it to undertake certain specific elements of the ecumenical vocation:

- animating and coordinating efforts for the coherence of the ecumenical movement;
- serving as a mediator among parties in conflict and as an advocate for groups who are unable to speak for themselves;
- being a seed-bed of ideas and a source of analysis, drawing on the rich experiences of its member churches;
- demonstrating the interconnections between the local and the global;
- speaking a prophetic word from the global perspective to address urgent issues of the day.

8. The fiftieth anniversary of the founding of the World Council of Churches is a fitting moment for the churches, at the dawning of a new millennium, to recommit themselves to the ecumenical vision and to deepen their participation in the WCC.

The governing bodies established by the WCC's constitution are the means of ensuring that the activities undertaken by the Council as an institution are attuned to the needs and concerns of its member churches and ecumenical partners.

They should function in ways that:

- ensure maximum representation and participation by the member churches, with policies set and decisions made in a transparent way;

- listen to the voices of all, not just to those whose culture, language, education or experience give them special advantages in the setting of a global organization;
- give priority to reflection and deliberation on the key issues facing the churches in the world today, rather than being dominated by institutional concerns;
- pay constant attention to the theological coherence and coordination of the WCC's activities, rather than being a place where particular interests and agendas lobby;
- establish and deepen relations with churches which are not WCC members but are open to ecumenical fellowship;
- stimulate those with leadership responsibilities in member churches to take up ecumenical concerns locally and to act ecumenically in their immediate context.

Appendix B

Members of the WCC Central Committee

Presidents

Dr Agnes Abuom
Anglican Church of Kenya

Right Rev. Jabez L. Bryce
Anglican Church in Aotearoa, New Zealand and Polynesia

H.E. Metropolitan Chrysostomos of Ephesus
Ecumenical Patriarchate [Turkey]

H.H. Patriarch Ignatius Zakka I Iwas
Syrian Orthodox Patriarchate of Antioch and All the East

Dr Moon Kyu Kang
Presbyterian Church in the Republic of Korea

Obispo Federico J. Pagura
Evangelical Methodist Church of Argentina

Rev. Dr Bernice Powell Jackson
United Church of Christ [USA]

Bischof Eberhardt Renz
Evangelical Church in Germany

Officers

Mrs Justice Sophia Adinyira*
Church of the Province of West Africa [Ghana]
Vice-moderator

*Member of the executive committee

His Holiness Aram I*
Armenian Apostolic Church (Holy See of Cilicia) [Lebanon]
Moderator

Dr Marion S. Best*
United Church of Canada
Vice-moderator

Rev. Dr Samuel Kobia*
Methodist Church in Kenya
General secretary

Members

Ms Inger Aasa-Marklund
Church of Sweden

Bishop Georges Abou Zakhm
Greek Orthodox Patriarchate of Antioch and All the East [Syria]

Ms Martha Aisi
Evangelical Lutheran Church of Papua New Guinea

Bishop Dr Hilarion Alfeyev*
Russian Orthodox Church

H.E. Metropolitan Ambrosios of Kalavryta and Aigealia
Church of Greece

H.E. Metropolitan Ambrosius of Helsinki
Orthodox Church of Finland

H.B. Archbishop Anastasios of Tirana, Durrës and All Albania
Orthodox Autocephalous Church of Albania

Mme Jeannette A. Aneye
*United Protestant Methodist Church
of the Ivory Coast*

Ms Keshini I. Arulendran
Church of Ceylon [Sri Lanka]

H.E. Metropolitan Athanasios Papas
of Heliopolis and Theira
Ecumenical Patriarchate [Turkey]

Mr Victor Avasi
Church of the Province of Uganda

Bishop Samuel R. Azariah
Church of Pakistan

Mme Louise Bakala Koumouno
Evangelical Church of the Congo

Rev. Canon Dr Trond Bakkevig
Church of Norway

H.E. Archbishop Aghan Baliozian
*Armenian Apostolic Church (Holy See
of Etchmiadzin) [Armenia]*

Pastor Oscar Bolioli
Methodist Church in Uruguay

Rev. Heike Bosien
Evangelical Church in Germany

Rev. Ruth Anne Bottoms
Baptist Union of Great Britain

Rev. Avedis Boynerian
*Union of the Armenian Evangelical
Churches in the Near East [Lebanon]*

Rt Rev. Tom Butler
Church of England

Rev. José Domingos Caetano
*Evangelical Pentecostal Mission
of Angola*

Mrs Selai Cati
Kiribati Protestant Church

Rev. Dr Simão Chamango
Presbyterian Church of Mozambique

Archpriest Vsevolod Chaplin
Russian Orthodox Church

Ms Iulia Corduneanu
Romanian Orthodox Church

Rev. Inamar Corrêa de Souza*
Episcopal Anglican Church of Brazil

Ms Lois McCullough Dauway
United Methodist Church [USA]

Rt Rev. Dr Govada Dyvasirvadam
Church of South India

Mrs Esther Malwine Edu-Yao
Evangelical Presbyterian Church, Ghana

Mrs Donnalie Edwards-Cabey*
*Church in the Province
of the West Indies [Bahamas]*

Rev. Dr Fernando Enns
Mennonite Church in Germany

Rt Rev. C. Christopher Epting
Episcopal Church in the USA

Obispo Aldo M. Etchegoyen
*Evangelical Methodist Church
of Argentina*

Ms Alice-Jean Finlay
Anglican Church of Canada

Pfr Serge Fornerod
Federation of Swiss Protestant Churches

183

Sra Manuela Fuentes de Capó
Spanish Evangelical Church

Dean Anders Gadegaard*
Evangelical Lutheran Church in Denmark

Prof. George Galitis
Church of Greece

Rev. Ying Gao
China Christian Council

Metropolitan Prof. Dr Gennadios
of Sassima*
Ecumenical Patriarchate [Turkey]

Rev. Fr Dr Kondothra M. George*
Malankara Orthodox Syrian Church [India]

Bischof Hans Gerny
Old Catholic Church of Switzerland

Ms Silva Ghazelian
*Armenian Apostolic Church (Holy See
of Etchmiadzin) [Armenia]*

Mrs Anne Glynn-Mackoul
*Greek Orthodox Patriarchate of Antioch
and All the East [USA]*

Rev. Iteffa Gobena*
*Ethiopian Evangelical Church
Mekane Yesus*

Eden Grace
*Religious Society of Friends – Friends
United Meeting [USA]*

Rev. Wesley Granberg-Michaelson
Reformed Church in America

Mr Gerald Green
Moravian Church in Nicaragua

Dr Richard A. Grounds
United Methodist Church [USA]

Archpriest Mikhail Gundiaev*
Russian Orthodox Church

Mme Titaua Hamblin
Maòhi Protestant Church

Rev. Dr Richard L. Hamm
*Christian Church – Disciples of Christ
[USA]*

Bischof Dr Martin Hein
Evangelical Church in Germany

Rev. Gregor Henderson
Uniting Church in Australia

Mrs Makiko Hirata
United Church of Christ in Japan

Rev. Wies L. J. Houweling
Protestant Church in the Netherlands

Mr Rasmus Hylleberg
Baptist Union of Denmark

Mr Wilhelm Harold Jap-A-Joe
Moravian Church in Suriname

Dr Priscilla Joseph Kouc
Sudan Council of Churches

Mrs Muna Kallas Malek
*Greek Orthodox Patriarchate of Antioch
and All the East [Syria]*

Rt Rev. Dr Jesse M. Kamau
*Presbyterian Church of East Africa
[Kenya]*

Mrs Carmencita Karagdag*
Philippine Independent Church

H.G. Bishop Dr Basilios Karayiannis
of Trimithus
Church of Cyprus

H.E. Archbishop Mor Cyril Aphrem
Karim*
*Syrian Orthodox Patriarchate of Antioch
and All the East*

Rev. Mari Kinnunen
Evangelical Lutheran Church of Finland

Rev. Dr Clifton Kirkpatrick*
Presbyterian Church (USA)

Very Rev. Leonid Kishkovsky*
Orthodox Church in America

Bischof D. Dr Christoph Klein
*Evangelical Church of the Augsburg
Confession in Romania*

Bischof Dr Rolf Koppe*
Evangelical Church in Germany

Ms Jana Krajciriková*
*Czechoslovak Hussite Church
[Czech Republic]*

Rev. Beate Kraus
United Methodist Church [USA]

Mrs Christa Kronshage
Evangelical Church in Germany

Oberkirchenrätin Marita Krüger
Evangelical Church in Germany

His Eminence Krystof
*Orthodox Church of the Czech Lands
and Slovakia [Czech Republic]*

Rev. Cibele Kuss
*Evangelical Church of Lutheran
Confession in Brazil*

Rev. Septemmy E. Lakawa*
*Protestant Church in South-East
Sulawesi [Indonesia]*

Prof. Dr Samuel Lee*
Presbyterian Church of Korea

H.E. Archbishop Makarios of Kenya
and Irinoupolis
*Greek Orthodox Patriarchate
of Alexandria and All Africa [Egypt]*

Mr Welly Esau Mandowen
*Evangelical Christian Church in Tanah
Papua [Indonesia]*

Dra Frieda Mangunsong
*Protestant Christian Batak Church
[Indonesia]*

Pasteur Marcel Manoël
Reformed Church of France

Rev. Pakoa Maraki
Presbyterian Church of Vanuatu

Rev. Dr Maake J. Masango*
*Uniting Presbyterian Church in Southern
Africa*

Rev. Erica Mathieson
Anglican Church of Australia

Rev. Jeffrey McKenzie
Jamaica Baptist Union

Rev. Dr Héctor Méndez
Presbyterian Reformed Church in Cuba

Bishop Mdimi Godfrey Mhogolo
Anglican Church of Tanzania

Dr Nenad Milosevic
*Serbian Orthodox Church
[Serbia and Montenegro]*

Mme Ngoy Mukuna Monique Misenga
*Presbyterian Community of Kinshasa
[Democratic Republic of Congo]*

Mrs Pragyan Mohanty-Yadav
Church of North India

Most Rev. Dr Barry Morgan
Church in Wales

Prof. Rev. Dr Nicolae Viorel Mosoiu
Romanian Orthodox Church

Mr Naboth M. Muchopa
Methodist Church of Great Britain

Bishop Cephas Z. Mukandi
Methodist Church in Zimbabwe

Bishop Ulises Muñoz Moraga
Pentecostal Church of Chile

Pasteur Elisée Musemakweli
Presbyterian Church of Rwanda

Mrs Patricia Mutumburanzou
Reformed Church in Zimbabwe

Rt Rev. John Mweresa Kivuli II
African Israel Nineveh Church [Kenya]

Ms Jennifer Nagel
Evangelical Lutheran Church in America

Archbishop John R.W. Neill
Church of Ireland

Ms Margarita Nelyubova
Russian Orthodox Church

Archbishop Nifon of Targoviste*
Romanian Orthodox Church

Ms Idah Njobvu
Reformed Church in Zambia

Mr Arthur Norman
Evangelical Lutheran Church in America

Rt Rev. Bernard Ntahoturi
Episcopal Church of Burundi

Archbishop Dr Rufus Ositelu
*Church of the Lord (Aladura) Worldwide
[Nigeria]*

Rev. Dr Jong-Wha Park
*Presbyterian Church in the Republic
of Korea*

Dr Vladan Perisic
*Serbian Orthodox Church
[Serbia and Montenegro]*

Dr Rubina Peroomian
*Armenian Apostolic Church (Holy See
of Cilicia) [Lebanon]*

Rev. Dr Tyrone Pitts
*Progressive National Baptist
Convention, Inc. [USA]*

Rev. Dr Staccato Powell
*African Methodist Episcopal Zion
Church [USA]*

Dr Despina Prassas
Ecumenical Patriarchate [Turkey]

Dr Aueh Quawas
Greek Orthodox Patriarchate of Jerusalem

Archbishop Remi J. Rabenirina
*Church of the Province of the
Indian Ocean [Madagascar]*

Mr Leonardo D. Ratuwalangon
*Kalimantan Evangelical Church
[Indonesia]*

Rev. Dr Bruce W. Robbins
United Methodist Church [USA]

Rev. John Haig Roberts
Methodist Church of New Zealand

Mme Jeannine Colette Rogier-Libbrecht
United Protestant Church of Belgium

Mr Georgy Roschin
Russian Orthodox Church

Mr Albert A.K. Samadder
Church of Bangladesh

Bishop Telmor Sartison
Evangelical Lutheran Church in Canada

Rev. Dr Robert Sawyer
Moravian Church in America

Dr Anna May Say Pa
Myanmar Baptist Convention

Rev. Ashley Seaman
Presbyterian Church (USA)

H.G. Bishop Serapion
Coptic Orthodox Church [Egypt]

Rev. Dr Natan Setiabudi
Indonesian Christian Church

Rev. Norman Shanks
Church of Scotland

Rev. Dr Hermen Shastri
Council of Churches of Malaysia

Ms Iveta Starcova
*Orthodox Church of the Czech Lands
and Slovakia [Czech Republic]*

Rev. Pawel Stefanowski
*Polish Autocephalous Orthodox Church
in Poland*

Bishop Michael Kehinde Stephen
Methodist Church Nigeria

Rev. Zoltán Tarr
Reformed Church in Hungary

Mrs Woraporn Tharawanich
Church of Christ in Thailand

Bishop Dr Zacharias Mar Theophilus*
*Mar Thoma Syrian Church of Malabar
[India]*

Rev. Jill Thornton
United Reformed Church [UK]

Mme Madeleine Sara Tiki-Koum (Soppo)
Evangelical Church of Cameroon

Rev. Stephan Titus
*United Congregational Church of
Southern Africa*

Bishop Dr Christ Saban Royan Topno
*United Evangelical Lutheran Church
in India*

Ms Chia-Chun (Annie) Tsai Kakun
Presbyterian Church in Taiwan

Rev. Dr Ilaitia Sevati Tuwere*
Methodist Church in Fiji

Rev. Lydia Veliko
United Church of Christ [USA]

Rev. Dr Cheryl H. Wade
American Baptist Churches in the USA

Rev. Dr Angelique Walker-Smith
National Baptist Convention USA, Inc.

Bishop Anba Youannes
Coptic Orthodox Church [Egypt]

Bishop McKinley Young*
*African Methodist Episcopal Church
[USA]*

Fr Melake Tabor Teshome Zerihun
Ethiopian Orthodox Tewahedo Church

During its 2002 meeting
in Geneva, the WCC
central committee selects
Porto Alegre, Brazil, as
the venue of the ninth
assembly to take place in
February 2006.

188

Member Churches
of the World Council of Churches

AFRICA

Africa Church [Nigeria]

Africa Inland Church – Sudan

African Christian Church and Schools [Kenya] *

African Church of the Holy Spirit [Kenya]

African Israel Nineveh Church [Kenya]

African Protestant Church [Cameroon] *

Anglican Church of Kenya

Anglican Church of Tanzania

Association of Evangelical Reformed Churches of Burkina Faso *

Association of Baptist Churches in Rwanda

Church of Christ – Light of the Holy Spirit [Democratic Republic of Congo]

Church of Christ in Congo – Anglican Community of Congo

Church of Christ in Congo – Baptist Community of Western Congo

Church of Christ in Congo – Community of Disciples of Christ

Church of Christ in Congo – Episcopal Baptist Community

Church of Christ in Congo – Evangelical Community

Church of Christ in Congo – Mennonite Community

Church of Christ in Congo – Presbyterian Community

Church of Christ in Congo – Presbyterian Community of Kinshasa

Church of Jesus Christ in Madagascar

Church of Jesus Christ on Earth by his Messenger Simon Kimbangu [Democratic
  Republic of Congo]

Church of Nigeria (Anglican Communion)

Church of the Brethren in Nigeria

Church of the Lord (Aladura) Worldwide [Nigeria]

Church of the Province of Central Africa [Zambia]

Church of the Province of Southern Africa [South Africa]

Church of the Province of the Indian Ocean [Madagascar]

Church of the Province of Uganda

Church of the Province of West Africa [Ghana]

Council of African Instituted Churches [South Africa]

Episcopal Church of Burundi

Episcopal Church of the Sudan

* *Associate member churches are indicated in this list by an asterisk.*

Eritrean Orthodox Tewahedo Church
Ethiopian Evangelical Church Mekane Yesus
Ethiopian Orthodox Tewahedo Church
Evangelical Baptist Church of Angola
Evangelical Church of Cameroon
Evangelical Church of Gabon
Evangelical Church of the Congo
Evangelical Congregational Church in Angola
Evangelical Lutheran Church in Congo
Evangelical Lutheran Church in Namibia
Evangelical Lutheran Church in Southern Africa [South Africa]
Evangelical Lutheran Church in Tanzania
Evangelical Lutheran Church in the Republic of Namibia
Evangelical Lutheran Church in Zimbabwe
Evangelical Lutheran Church of Ghana
Evangelical Pentecostal Mission of Angola
Evangelical Presbyterian Church in South Africa
Evangelical Presbyterian Church of Togo
Evangelical Presbyterian Church, Ghana
Evangelical Reformed Church of Angola
Harrist Church [Côte d'Ivoire]

Kenya Evangelical Lutheran Church *
Lesotho Evangelical Church
Lutheran Church in Liberia
Malagasy Lutheran Church
Methodist Church in Kenya
Methodist Church in Zimbabwe
Methodist Church Nigeria
Methodist Church of Southern Africa
Methodist Church of Togo
Methodist Church Sierra Leone
Methodist Church, Ghana
Moravian Church in South Africa
Native Baptist Church of Cameroon
Nigerian Baptist Convention
Presbyterian Church in Cameroon
Presbyterian Church in the Sudan
Presbyterian Church of Africa
Presbyterian Church of Cameroon
Presbyterian Church of East Africa
Presbyterian Church of Ghana
Presbyterian Church of Mozambique *
Presbyterian Church of Nigeria

Presbyterian Church of Rwanda
Presbytery of Liberia *
Protestant Church of Algeria *
Protestant Evangelical Church of Guinea
Protestant Methodist Church of Benin
Protestant Methodist Church of the Ivory Coast
Province of the Episcopal Church of Rwanda
Provinces of the Moravian Church in Tanzania
Reformed Church in Zambia
Reformed Church in Zimbabwe
Reformed Church of Christ in Nigeria
Reformed Presbyterian Church of Equatorial Guinea *
Union of Baptist Churches of Cameroon
United Church of Christ in Zimbabwe
United Church of Zambia
United Congregational Church of Southern Africa [South Africa]
United Evangelical Church "Anglican Communion in Angola"
Uniting Presbyterian Church in Southern Africa [South Africa]
Uniting Reformed Church in Southern Africa [South Africa]

ASIA

Anglican Church in Aotearoa, New Zealand and Polynesia
Anglican Church of Australia
Anglican Church of Korea
Anglican Communion in Japan
Associated Churches of Christ in New Zealand
Bangladesh Baptist Church Sangha
Baptist Union of New Zealand
Batak Christian Community Church (GPKB) [Indonesia] *
Bengal-Orissa-Bihar Baptist Convention [India] *
China Christian Council
Christian Church of Central Sulawesi (GKST) [Indonesia]
Christian Church of Sumba (GKS) [Indonesia]
Christian Evangelical Church in Minahasa (GMIM) [Indonesia]
Christian Evangelical Church in Sangihe Talaud (GMIST) [Indonesia]
Christian Protestant Angkola Church (GKPA) [Indonesia]
Christian Protestant Church in Indonesia (GKPI) [Indonesia]
Church of Bangladesh *
Church of Ceylon [Sri Lanka]
Church of Christ in Thailand
Church of North India
Church of Pakistan

Church of South India
Church of the Province of Myanmar
Churches of Christ in Australia
Convention of Philippine Baptist Churches
East Java Christian Church (GKJW) [Indonesia]
Episcopal Church in the Philippines
Evangelical Christian Church in Halmahera [Indonesia]
Evangelical Christian Church in Tanah Papua [Indonesia]
Evangelical Methodist Church in the Philippines
Hong Kong Council of the Church of Christ in China
Indonesian Christian Church (GKI)
Indonesian Christian Church (HKI)
Javanese Christian Churches (GKJ) [Indonesia]
Kalimantan Evangelical Church (GKE) [Indonesia]
Karo Batak Protestant Church (GBKP) [Indonesia]
Korean Christian Church in Japan *
Korean Methodist Church
Malankara Orthodox Syrian Church [India]
Mar Thoma Syrian Church of Malabar [India]
Mara Evangelical Church [Myanmar] *
Methodist Church in India
Methodist Church in Indonesia
Methodist Church in Malaysia
Methodist Church in Singapore *
Methodist Church of New Zealand
Methodist Church Sri Lanka
Methodist Church, Upper Myanmar
Myanmar Baptist Convention
Nias Protestant Christian Church (BNKP) [Indonesia]
Orthodox Church in Japan
Pasundan Christian Church (GKP) [Indonesia]
Philippine Independent Church
Presbyterian Church in Taiwan
Presbyterian Church in the Republic of Korea
Presbyterian Church of Aotearoa New Zealand
Presbyterian Church of Korea
Presbyterian Church of Pakistan
Protestant Christian Batak Church (HKBP) [Indonesia]
Protestant Christian Church in Bali (GKPB) [Indonesia] *
Protestant Church in Indonesia (GPI)
Protestant Church in Sabah (PCS) [Malaysia]
Protestant Church in South-East Sulawesi (GPST) [Indonesia]
Protestant Church in the Moluccas (GPM) [Indonesia]

Protestant Church in Timor Lorosa'e
Protestant Church in Western Indonesia (GPIB)
Protestant Evangelical Church in Timor (GMIT) [Indonesia]
Samavesam of Telugu Baptist Churches [India]
Simalungun Protestant Christian Church (GKPS) [Indonesia]
Toraja Church [Indonesia]
United Church of Christ in Japan
United Church of Christ in the Philippines
United Evangelical Lutheran Churches in India
Uniting Church in Australia

CARIBBEAN

Baptist Convention of Haïti
Church in the Province of the West Indies [Bahamas]
Jamaica Baptist Union
Methodist Church in Cuba *
Methodist Church in the Caribbean and the Americas
Methodist Church of Porto Rico *
Moravian Church in Jamaica
Moravian Church in Suriname
Moravian Church, Eastern West Indies Province [Antigua and Barbuda]
Presbyterian Church in Trinidad and Tobago
Presbyterian Reformed Church in Cuba *
United Church in Jamaica and the Cayman Islands [Jamaica]
United Protestant Church [Curaçao] *

EUROPE

Armenian Apostolic Church (Etchmiadzin)
Baptist Union of Denmark
Baptist Union of Great Britain
Baptist Union of Hungary
Catholic Diocese of the Old Catholics in Germany
Church in Wales
Church of England
Church of Greece
Church of Ireland
Church of Norway
Church of Scotland
Church of Sweden
Church of the Augsburg Confession of Alsace and Lorraine [France]
Czechoslovak Hussite Church

193

Ecumenical Patriarchate [Turkey]
Estonian Evangelical Lutheran Church
European Continental Province of the Moravian Church [Netherlands]
Evangelical Baptist Union of Italy *
Evangelical Church in Germany
Evangelical Church of Czech Brethren
Evangelical Church of the Augsburg and Helvetic Confessions in Austria
Evangelical Church of the Augsburg Confession in Poland
Evangelical Church of the Augsburg Confession in Romania
Evangelical Church of the Augsburg Confession in Slovakia
Evangelical Lutheran Church in Denmark
Evangelical Lutheran Church of Finland
Evangelical Lutheran Church of France
Evangelical Lutheran Church of Iceland
Evangelical Lutheran Church of Latvia
Evangelical Methodist Church of Italy
Evangelical Presbyterian Church of Portugal *
Evangelical-Lutheran Church from Romania
Federation of Swiss Protestant Churches
Greek Evangelical Church
Latvian Evangelical Lutheran Church Abroad [Germany]
Lusitanian Church of Portugal *
Lutheran Church of Hungary
Mennonite Church Germany
Mennonite Church in the Netherlands
Methodist Church of Great Britain
Methodist Church in Ireland
Mission Covenant Church of Sweden
Moravian Church in Great Britain and Ireland
Old Catholic Church of Austria
Old Catholic Church of Switzerland
Old Catholic Church of the Netherlands
Old Catholic Mariavite Church in Poland
Orthodox Autocephalous Church of Albania
Orthodox Church of Finland
Orthodox Church of the Czech Lands and Slovakia
Polish Autocephalous Orthodox Church
Polish Catholic Church in Poland
Presbyterian Church of Wales
Protestant Church in the Netherlands
Reformed Christian Church in Slovakia
Reformed Christian Church in Serbia and Montenegro
Reformed Church in Hungary

Reformed Church of Alsace and Lorraine [France]
Reformed Church of France
Reformed Church of Romania
Remonstrant Brotherhood [Netherlands]
Romanian Orthodox Church
Russian Orthodox Church
Scottish Episcopal Church [United Kingdom]
Serbian Orthodox Church [Serbia and Montenegro]
Silesian Evangelical Church of the Augsburg Confession in Czechoslovakia
Slovak Evangelical Church of the Augsburg Confession in Serbia and Montenegro
Spanish Evangelical Church
Spanish Reformed Episcopal Church *
Union of Welsh Independents [United Kingdom]
United Free Church of Scotland [United Kingdom]
United Protestant Church of Belgium
United Reformed Church [United Kingdom]
Waldensian Church [Italy]

LATIN AMERICA

Anglican Church of the Southern Cone of America [Argentina]
Baptist Association of El Salvador *
Baptist Convention of Nicaragua
Bolivian Evangelical Lutheran Church *
Christian Biblical Church [Argentina] *
Christian Reformed Church of Brazil
Church of God [Argentina] *
Church of the Disciples of Christ [Argentina] *
Episcopal Anglican Church of Brazil
Evangelical Church of Lutheran Confession in Brazil
Evangelical Church of the River Plate [Argentina]
Evangelical Lutheran Church in Chile
Evangelical Methodist Church in Bolivia *
Evangelical Methodist Church in Uruguay *
Evangelical Methodist Church of Argentina
Evangelical Methodist Church of Costa Rica
Free Pentecostal Mission Church of Chile
Methodist Church in Brazil
Methodist Church of Chile *
Methodist Church of Mexico
Methodist Church of Peru *
Moravian Church in Nicaragua
Pentecostal Church of Chile

Pentecostal Mission Church
Presbyterian Church of Columbia *
Salvadorean Lutheran Synod *
United Evangelical Lutheran Church [Argentina] *
United Presbyterian Church of Brazil *

MIDDLE EAST

Armenian Apostolic Church (Cilicia) [Lebanon]
Church of Cyprus
Coptic Orthodox Church [Egypt]
Episcopal Church in Jerusalem and the Middle East [Israel]
Greek Orthodox Patriarchate of Alexandria and All Africa [Egypt]
Greek Orthodox Patriarchate of Antioch and All the East [Syria]
Greek Orthodox Patriarchate of Jerusalem
National Evangelical Synod of Syria and Lebanon [Lebanon]
Synod of the Evangelical Church of Iran
Synod of the Nile of the Evangelical Church [Egypt]
Syrian Orthodox Patriarchate of Antioch and All the East
Union of the Armenian Evangelical Churches in the Near East [Lebanon]

NORTH AMERICA

African Methodist Episcopal Church [USA]
African Methodist Episcopal Zion Church [USA]
American Baptist Churches in the USA
Anglican Church of Canada
Apostolic Catholic Assyrian Church of the East-N. A. Diocese [USA]
Canadian Yearly Meeting of the Religious Society of Friends
Christian Church (Disciples of Christ) [USA]
Christian Church (Disciples of Christ) in Canada
Christian Methodist Episcopal Church [USA]
Church of the Brethren [USA]
Episcopal Church in the USA
Estonian Evangelical Lutheran Church Abroad [Canada]
Evangelical Lutheran Church in America
Evangelical Lutheran Church in Canada
Hungarian Reformed Church in America
International Council of Community Churches [USA]
International Evangelical Church [USA]
Moravian Church in America [USA]
National Baptist Convention of America
National Baptist Convention USA, Inc.

Orthodox Church in America [USA]

Polish National Catholic Church [USA]

Presbyterian Church (USA)

Presbyterian Church in Canada

Progressive National Baptist Convention, Inc. [USA]

Reformed Church in America [USA]

Religious Society of Friends – Friends General Conference [USA]

Religious Society of Friends – Friends United Meeting [USA]

United Church of Canada

United Church of Christ [USA]

United Methodist Church [USA]

PACIFIC

Church of Melanesia

Church of Niue [Niue Island]

Congregational Christian Church in American Samoa

Congregational Christian Church in Samoa

Cook Islands Christian Church

Evangelical Church in New Caledonia and the Loyalty Isles [New Caledonia]

Evangelical Lutheran Church of Papua New Guinea

Free Wesleyan Church of Tonga (Methodist Church in Tonga)

Kiribati Protestant Church

Maòhi Protestant Church

Methodist Church in Fiji

Methodist Church in Samoa

Presbyterian Church of Vanuatu

Tuvalu Christian Church

United Church in Papua New Guinea

United Church in Solomon Islands

United Church of Christ-Congregational in the Marshall Islands

198

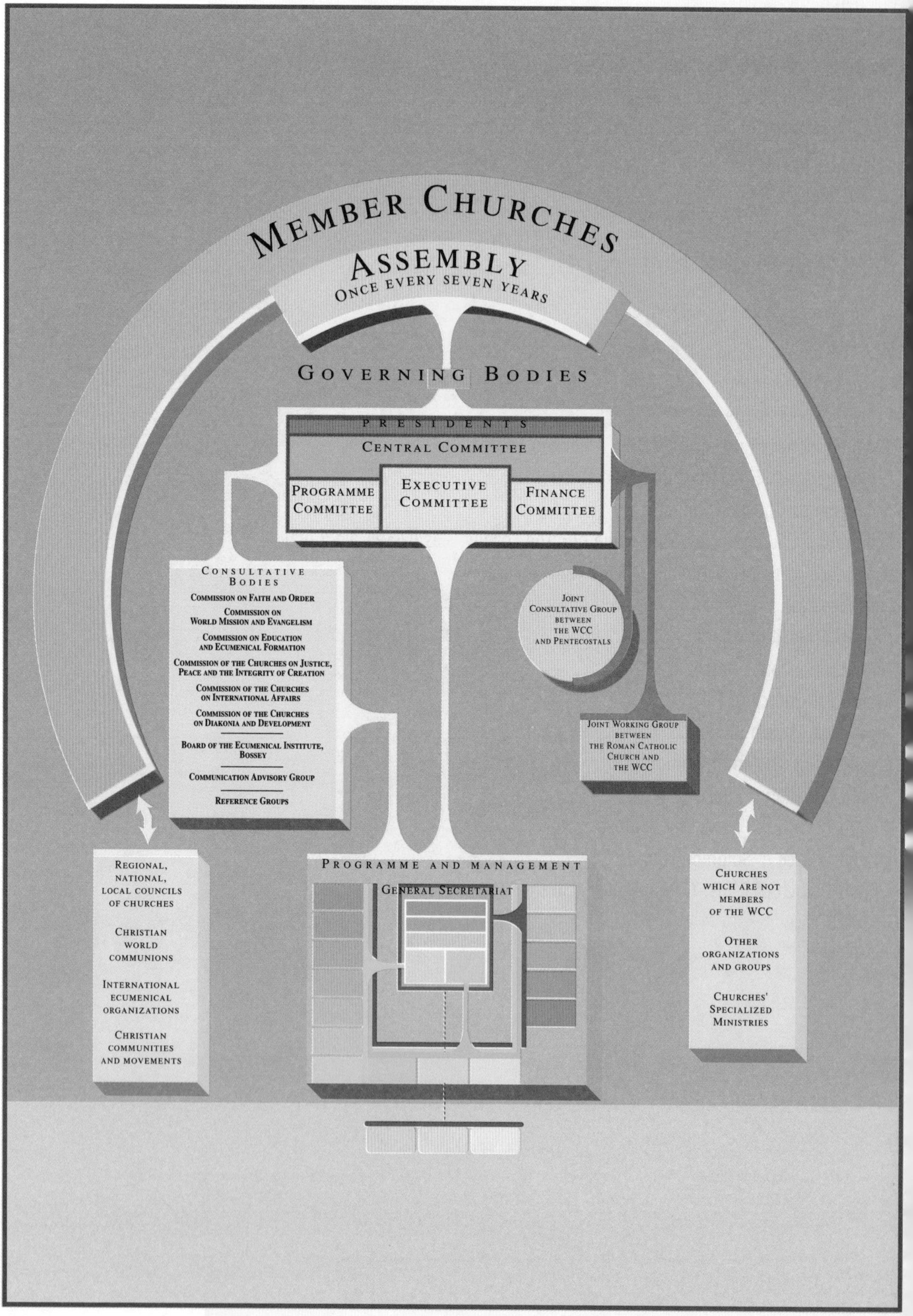

MEMBER CHURCHES

ASSEMBLY
ONCE EVERY SEVEN YEARS

GOVERNING BODIES

PRESIDENTS

CENTRAL COMMITTEE

PROGRAMME COMMITTEE

EXECUTIVE COMMITTEE

FINANCE COMMITTEE

CONSULTATIVE BODIES

COMMISSION ON FAITH AND ORDER

COMMISSION ON WORLD MISSION AND EVANGELISM

COMMISSION ON EDUCATION AND ECUMENICAL FORMATION

COMMISSION OF THE CHURCHES ON JUSTICE, PEACE AND THE INTEGRITY OF CREATION

COMMISSION OF THE CHURCHES ON INTERNATIONAL AFFAIRS

COMMISSION OF THE CHURCHES ON DIAKONIA AND DEVELOPMENT

BOARD OF THE ECUMENICAL INSTITUTE, BOSSEY

COMMUNICATION ADVISORY GROUP

REFERENCE GROUPS

JOINT CONSULTATIVE GROUP BETWEEN THE WCC AND PENTECOSTALS

JOINT WORKING GROUP BETWEEN THE ROMAN CATHOLIC CHURCH AND THE WCC

REGIONAL, NATIONAL, LOCAL COUNCILS OF CHURCHES

CHRISTIAN WORLD COMMUNIONS

INTERNATIONAL ECUMENICAL ORGANIZATIONS

CHRISTIAN COMMUNITIES AND MOVEMENTS

PROGRAMME AND MANAGEMENT

GENERAL SECRETARIAT

CHURCHES WHICH ARE NOT MEMBERS OF THE WCC

OTHER ORGANIZATIONS AND GROUPS

CHURCHES' SPECIALIZED MINISTRIES

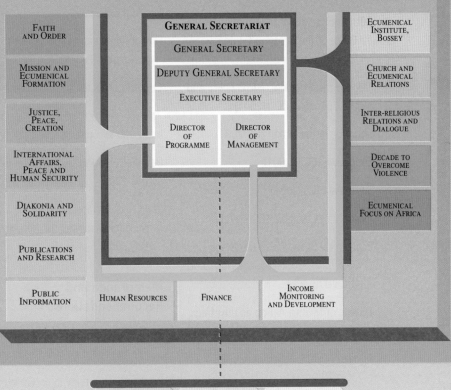

PROGRAMME AND MANAGEMENT

GENERAL SECRETARIAT

GENERAL SECRETARY

DEPUTY GENERAL SECRETARY

EXECUTIVE SECRETARY

DIRECTOR OF PROGRAMME

DIRECTOR OF MANAGEMENT

FAITH AND ORDER

MISSION AND ECUMENICAL FORMATION

JUSTICE, PEACE, CREATION

INTERNATIONAL AFFAIRS, PEACE AND HUMAN SECURITY

DIAKONIA AND SOLIDARITY

PUBLICATIONS AND RESEARCH

PUBLIC INFORMATION

HUMAN RESOURCES

FINANCE

INCOME MONITORING AND DEVELOPMENT

ECUMENICAL INSTITUTE, BOSSEY

CHURCH AND ECUMENICAL RELATIONS

INTER-RELIGIOUS RELATIONS AND DIALOGUE

DECADE TO OVERCOME VIOLENCE

ECUMENICAL FOCUS ON AFRICA

ECUMENICAL ADVOCACY ALLIANCE

ACTION BY CHURCHES TOGETHER

ECUMENICAL NEWS INTERNATIONAL

Appendix E

Public Issues Adopted by the WCC Central and Executive Committees,

1999-February 2005

Statements

Chechnya (EC 2000)

50th Anniversary of the Creation of the Office of the UN High Commissioner for Refugees (UNHCR) (EC 9/2000)

Nuclear Disarmament, NATO Policy and the Churches (CC 1/2001)

Situation in the Sudan (CC 2001)

Zimbabwe (EC 9/2001)

South Asia (CC 2002)

Violence in Colombia (CC 2002)

Ecumenical Response to the Israeli-Palestinian Conflict in the Holy Land (CC 2002)

Threats of Military Action against Iraq (CC 2002)

Against Military Action in Iraq (EC 2/2003)

Iraq (CC 2003)

Liberia (CC 2003)

Europe (CC 2003)

The Wall in the Occupied Palestinian Territories and Israel's Annexation of Palestinian Territory (EC 2/2004)

The Nuclear Non-Proliferation Treaty, NPT (EC 2/2004)

Sudan (EC 8/2004)

Human Rights and Languages of Indigenous Peoples (CC 2005)

Countries Affected by the Tsunami (CC 2005)

International Criminal Court (CC 2005)

Detainees Held at Guantanamo Bay (CC 2005)

Iraq Crisis: Enhancing Peace, Accountability and the Rule of Law (CC 2005)

Memoranda and Recommendations

Response to Armed Conflict and International Law (CC 1999)

Practising Hospitality in an Era of New Forms of Migration (CC 2005)

Minutes

Nigeria (CC 1999)

Jerusalem (CC 1999)

Indonesia (CC 1999)

Peace and Reconciliation between
  Ethiopia and Eritrea (CC 1999)

Cyprus (EC 2000)

Indonesia (EC 2000)

Situation in the Holy Land after the
  Outbreak of the Second Palestinian
  Uprising (CC 2001)

Colombia (CC 2001)

Cyprus (CC 2001)

Indonesia (CC 2001)

Peace Process in Sudan (CC 2002)

Tragedy of 11 September 2001 and the
  Implications of the US Government's
  Response (CC 2002)

Re-negotiation of the Compacts of Free
  Association between the USA and the
  Federated States of Micronesia and
  the Republic of the Marshall Islands
  (CC 2002)

Cyprus (EC 2/2003)

Peace Process in Sri Lanka (EC 2/2003)

The Responsibility to Protect: Ethical and
  Theological Reflection (CC2003)

Cyprus (CC 2003)

Occupied Palestinian Territories
  (CC 2003)

Zimbabwe (CC 2003)

Sudan (EC 2/2004)

India/Pakistan Composite Dialogue
  (EC 2/2004)

Economic Measures for Peace in
  Israel/Palestine (CC 2005)

Other

Resolution on Jerusalem Final Status
  Negotiations (EC 9/2000)

Uprooted People (EC 1/2001)

Study Document on the Protection of
  Endangered Populations in Situations
  of Armed Violence: Towards an
  Ecumenical Ethical Approach (CC
  2001)

Resolution on the Palestinian-Israeli
  Conflict (EC 9/2001)

Letter to the Churches in the US
  Following 9/11 (EC 9/2001)

201

Executive Summary

of the *Pre-assembly*
Programme
Evaluation

28 June 2005

Including Recommendations
Adopted by the Central Committee
of the World Council of Churches
February 2005

1. The evaluation process

1.1 The evaluation terms of reference

For the first time in its history, the WCC has engaged in a major assessment of its programmatic work with and for the global fellowship from the perspective of the constituency.[1] The executive committee decided on the terms of reference in February 2004 and nominated four persons, Marion Best, William Ogara, Sylvia Raulo and Georges Tsetsis, to carry out the evaluation process. The current global ecumenical context as described in the Harare to Porto Alegre report needs to be taken into account in reading this summary.

1.2 Evaluation methodology and limitations

The information-gathering process included listening to the constituency, both the voices and the silence. Questionnaires and interviews, both with individuals and groups, were the methods used. Input was received in one way or another from about one half of the member churches representing every region. In all there was contact with over 300 individuals from the constituency during the data-gathering processes including some regional group interviews and 59 in-depth individual interviews. The team also recognized the active and self-critical participation of the staff leadership group[2] and staff programme teams who were interviewed twice during the process.

There was great convergence on findings in general, and during the February 2005 central committee meeting representatives of the member churches indicated that the report "rang true" from their perspective. Although evaluation of programme priority setting and decision-making by governing bodies was not part of our mandate, it should be noted that self-evaluation by programme committee and central committee indicate a desire for improvement in this area of their work. A full 40-page report has gone to the assembly programme guidelines committee to assist them in their work, including a short evaluation of each individual programme, and is available on *http://www.oik-oumene.org/GEN_8_Report_on_the_Pre-A.676.0.html* .

While our team has recognized limitations in this evaluation process, this assessment of WCC programmes has brought significant information from the constituency about the image of the WCC, the reception of its programmes, the issues that are most pressing for them and the methodologies that they found most useful. Many who responded applauded the WCC for undertaking such an exercise and it was seen as a desire on the part of the Council to be transparent and to seek improvements in a number of areas.

2. *Summary of key findings*

2.1 *Meeting overall programme goals*

To what extent have the programmes implemented during the period of evaluation **met the overall goals** set by the last assembly and the subsequent programme policy framework defined by the central committee and by the commissions/advisory bodies?

"It is difficult to understand what the overall goals are; it seems there are several different layers." [3]

Main findings

Most respondents indicated they were not familiar with the overall or specific programme goals. Although our evaluation team assumed the overarching vision for the work of the Council is the Common Understanding and Vision (CUV) document,[4] many respondents said the WCC's vision is "blurred". Having a clearly articulated vision is essential for setting clear overall goals for the programmatic work.

While they were not able to name specific programme goals, most had a general knowledge of the issues the Harare assembly identified and to which the Council had given its attention. The issues most often named were violence, HIV/AIDS, economic justice, focus on Africa, and the relations of the Orthodox churches and others within the WCC. All these issues had been subjects of discussion during the eighth assembly and they continued to be identified as pertinent.

Harare programme directions were generally assessed to be too wide-ranging especially since dwindling human and financial resources have resulted in the WCC being able to achieve less. Repeatedly we heard that the Council must do less and do it well. Priorities have to be set based upon a clearly articulated vision and through determining what a global body, taking the funding realities into consideration, best does.

Team conclusions

- Appreciation was expressed for what had been achieved especially in the light of financial restraints and staff reductions. Achievement of goals, when general knowledge was low, was interpreted by the respondents as equalling ownership: this is when programmes are being used and/or affirmed by their own constituencies.
- Respondents were able to identify a number of issues that were highlighted at the eighth assembly and are still considered timely and there was general satisfaction that WCC is working with those, although they were not able to identify specific programmes.
- The lack of a clear overarching vision has made it difficult to set understandable overall goals for the programme work and to set priorities.

- The governing bodies[5] have difficulty in setting programme priorities and in carrying out their role of initiating, monitoring and terminating programmes, and this calls for a more flexible and transparent programme framework.
- Because the Harare assembly and the subsequent central committee meetings were unable to clearly articulate overall programme goals and set priorities, the result has been that the WCC is trying to do more than it can effectively handle given the extent of its financial and human resources. Guidelines need to be given for setting programme priorities following the ninth assembly.

2.2 Relevance, pertinence and significance

To what extent are the programmes relevant, pertinent and significant in relation to the priority needs of the constituency, and how were these programmes able to adjust to changing world contexts and emerging needs?

"The relevance and ownership of programmes are weakened when it is perceived that it is a separate agenda from the normal life of the churches."

Main findings

The issues of relevance, pertinence and significance were most often interpreted by the respondents as relating to the importance of a particular issue for the constituency, the creative methods used by a particular WCC programme, and the extent to which these had been combined to create a programme that the churches were able to relate to easily, could use/draw inspiration and ideas from for their own reality, and linked them with other churches and actors around the globe.

Some specific programmes were mentioned and the evaluation identified characteristics of these programmes in order to discern what makes a WCC programme relevant and significant to various parts of the constituency. It is recognized that, while many WCC programmes are designed and implemented to meet the needs of member churches, there is also the need for member churches to be challenged and horizons broadened by what the WCC offers.

Specific programmes identified in this area of inquiry as relevant to the constituency were the Decade to Overcome Violence; the work of the Bossey Ecumenical Institute in ecumenical formation; ethics of life and alternatives to globalization, especially in the area of economic justice; HIV/AIDS; uprootedness; and the special focus on Africa.

Advocacy at the global level in relation to a number of issues was mentioned as an important and fundamental function of the WCC. The Ecumenical Disability Advocacy Network and Indigenous peoples programmes are examples of work centred outside Geneva that are considered significant and point to the need for more thoroughly evaluating the potential in this type of networking.

The Special Commission on Orthodox Participation in the WCC was deemed significant and relevant as an example of activity that responded to a particular situation and need of the Council and its constituency. It is an example of the Council finding a way to discuss and formulate new ways of working in the midst of difficult and divisive issues. While it started mainly as a concern for the regions where the Orthodox constituency is strong, the results have a potential to reshape relations within the whole fellowship.

Team conclusions
- The programmes most often identified as relevant and significant by respondents were the ones that were addressing issues that were urgent or timely in their context or deemed fundamental for the mission of the Council.
- There are clear characteristics for the programmes that were most often mentioned: in addition to the issues, the work done has been done in cooperation with the churches in the regions and had a clear ownership, the WCC's role was one of facilitating, coordinating, accompanying, networking, connecting and/or capacity-building
- Solid theological frameworks are needed for the work being undertaken.
- Those with high relevance were also often programmes with a clear direction and scope, and communicated well.

2.3 Ownership and impact of programmes
*To what extent have the programmes been owned and used by the constituency, and have they produced a **lasting or significant impact** (positive or negative, intended or not) in the life of the churches and of the people they serve?*

"To be positive, one should say that during the last few years the Council has shown more awareness and concern to make an impact, make a difference."

Main findings
Impact is not easily measured within such a short period (effectively the years 1999-2003), as it is by nature long-term. In this respect, it was interesting to note that when answering impact, people would refer to such past programmes or activities of the WCC as the Decade of Churches in Solidarity with Women; Baptism, Eucharist and Ministry; the long record of human-rights work in Latin America; the Programme to Combat Racism – all still perceived as impacting the life of the churches with the profound changes they brought with them.

Ownership and use of programmes is a major factor for impact and many in the churches were self-critical of their lack of involvement. Introducing new subjects, clear communication and time-lines were other important elements. There had to be a clear role of the churches either as initiators (acute problems facing churches), implementers (being part of the execution of the programme or part of an advocacy effort) or by challenging their own ways of working/helping them address an acute need. The programmes needed to reach grassroots and be empowering. The language and accessible ways of addressing issues were mentioned as important elements in spreading information about programmes. The dominance of English puts limitations on who is reached. Many programmes have positive side effects in terms of giving people involved a more global, open identity and changed relationships but this is not documented or analyzed and an important dimension of the programmes is lost.

While there is more awareness of the need for improvements in programme planning, the WCC still lacks a fully functioning planning, monitoring and evaluation mechanism. Such a mechanism would include goal-oriented plans with objectives and indicators on impact and systematic follow-up and processing of feedback. Follow-up is especially important in order to learn from both successes and failures.

Team conclusions
- Planning for a time scope of several years is important for any desired lasting impacts.
- There is an urgent need to develop further the existing programme management mechanism and put into place a functioning planning, monitoring and evaluation mechanism and indicators to assess any measurable impact (or even results

giving impact in the future) of the present work. This is also needed to track unwanted or unexpected impact of programmes.
- Communication about the programmes and their goals and objectives is the key element in spreading the impact beyond those directly linked to programmes, and in the majority of cases it needs to be strengthened.
- Resolving the dilemma of commitment in principle but on the other hand a lack of interest and ownership by many member churches is another challenge (including a lack of financial commitment). A key issue to be addressed is how to set loose the existing potential of involvement in the member churches.
- The greater the role of the local churches, the greater the impact. This needs to challenge the programme designs if the WCC is really to make a difference.

2.4 Impact of programmes on strengthening the fellowship

*To what extent has each individual programme **served the CUV process**, facilitating the cooperation among the churches and offering involvement and commitment to the constituency, and has the **overall impact strengthened the fellowship?***

"Fellowship must go beyond live-and-let-live. It is more than warming up ourselves. It must enable us to change where change is deemed essential for the achievement of our mission."

Main findings

The document "Towards a Common Understanding and Vision" contains the guiding vision of the WCC upon which its mission and programmatic life is based. It declares that the WCC is a fellowship of churches that desires to move to visible unity and to carry out their common calling through witness and service to the world. Given the foundational nature of the CUV, it was surprising to discover in the evaluation that for most of the respondents the CUV was either unknown or has remained a historical document.

The majority said the work of the Special Commission had contributed to deepening the fellowship. There are many voices anticipating that the Council's move to consensus decision-making will increase understanding, build trust and deepen relationships within the fellowship. On the other hand, there is also concern about the extent to which the prophetic role of the Council can be safeguarded in the light of this change. Other means affirmed for deepening and strengthening the fellowship included team visits, "Living Letters" with the emphasis on church-to-church visits, visits by the general secretary and WCC staff teams.

The CUV also puts emphasis on widening the fellowship, and there have been a number of initiatives in this area since the eighth assembly for which many expressed appreciation. However there is a creative tension as WCC tries both to deepen and widen the fellowship. Some fear resources given to widening the fellowship will mean less for deepening it. There needs to be more intentional and strategic planning with both the regional ecumenical organizations and the Christian world communions. Programme work needs to be assessed not in isolation but collectively and move towards a "knitting together" of the programmes by the various players.

Team conclusions

- If the CUV is to remain the vision statement of the WCC, it needs to be clearly rearticulated and interpreted, the language simplified and the document widely shared.
- The majority of respondents said the Special Commission contributed to deepening the fellowship.
- Processes and methods that contribute to deepening the fellowship include creating "ecumenical space", church-to-church visits, visits by WCC staff, capacity-building and establishing and nurturing networks, hence enhancing the relational side, and several new initiatives are helping to widen the fellowship.
- Human resources are being stretched as the Council works on both deepening and widening the fellowship. Ways to utilize the time and talents of individuals and churches beyond WCC staff need to be increased.
- While affirming the reconfiguration process, some said its relationship to the CUV needs to be clarified.
- In order to strengthen the fellow-

ship, the WCC needs to examine how programme work is designed together with other actors. There is a need for a clear intentional strategy for involvement in each of the regions following analysis and a revisioning of roles.

• The WCC has done well to hold the fellowship together in the midst of significant challenges. The struggle is, however, far from over given the demands by the constituency and the WCC has to invest resources in creating space for fellowship to continue. There is a value in staying together even in difficult times.

2.5 WCC methods and ways of working in relation to programmes

"WCC methodology? The first thing that comes to my mind is an elderly gentleman reading his paper to us."

Main findings

Communication within and beyond the constituency was the most often cited area of problems and potentialities. The use of alternative pedagogical approaches and an overall ecumenical formation aspect in all the work is crucial. In this respect the WCC is perceived as lacking competence in the use of innovative methodologies.

Meetings, consultations and conferences dominate the picture. While their importance in creating personal relations and human interaction are still valued, they are too often perceived as didactically archaic and seen as isolated events without a process of preparation and follow-up.

There are additional issues that need to be noted in the strategic follow-up of those who participate in WCC-related events. They often feel they do not have enough information, but an equally important challenge is that they do not always know how to use the information they have and how to disseminate it in an effective way. Lack of preparation and follow-up was not only identified as a WCC problem but were acknowledged with self-criticism.

Team conclusions

• A more systematic analysis of the methods used in some programmes with the successful record of involving the constituency e.g. through studies, research, sharing staff, visits to churches is an important element when rethinking the methods used by the Council.

• Communication of the programmes needs to be built into the design of the programme and the overall area of communication needs to be strengthened for the Council.

• Meetings and gatherings need to be linked to clearly outlined processes seen in the frame of continuous ecumenical formation.

• Programme designs need to be based on involving the constituency at all levels.

• The use of different methodologies needs to be looked at strategically and the choice based on core functions, such as strengthening the fellowship.

• The use of commission and committee members, participants and members of governing and advisory bodies in advocating and communicating the fellowship should be systematically thought through and looked at from a strategic point of view.

3. *Overall assessments of programmes and recommendations*

While our team has recognized limitations in this evaluation process, this assessment of WCC programmes has brought significant information from the constituency about the image of the WCC, the reception of its programmes, the issues that are most pressing for them and the methodologies they found most useful. Many respondents congratulated the WCC for undertaking the evaluation and for seeking transparency and improvements in a number of areas. Our team acknowledges the active and self critical participation of the leadership group and programme staff teams in this endeavour.

Our analysis of the results in surveys and interviews points to the need for new and different ways of thinking and structuring the programme work. If the CUV is intended to provide the stated vision for the WCC, it needs to be the key element in shaping the programme work.

There is a need for the WCC to implement systematic planning, monitoring and evaluation mechanisms with clear objectives, indicators and specific follow-up. Otherwise it is difficult to assess the lasting and significant impact of particular programmes.

With some notable exceptions the programme work at present is perceived as having limited relevance and impact and hence has limited ownership in the constituency.

Those programmes identified as being most relevant and significant with the highest ownership by the churches are ones where the issues being addressed are timely. The programmes most often commended were also those where they had been able to interconnect with regional, national or local initiatives. Some of these were regionally based and some had very light structure.

With this in mind, a flexible programme structure is needed to address the rapidly changing environment. This includes a transparent and accountable way to initiate, reformulate and terminate programmes. The WCC will need to play many different roles in the programme work such as facilitating, coordinating, convening, connecting, listening, accompanying and capacity-building. The classical programme divisions still found in the Council do not resonate with many churches especially in the South who want the WCC to accompany them in mission, education and diakonia in an inte-

211

gral way as they themselves do. Building and nurturing relationships and communication were identified as key elements that must be attended to in all the programmes, in order to overcome the distance between the constituency and the WCC. Language appeared frequently as a limiting factor in utilizing resources, due to the predominant use of English as well as what is referred to as "Eurocentric" language and methodologies.

There was wide acknowledgment of the dedication of the staff working with reduced human and financial resources. Repeatedly there was an appeal for the WCC in the light of funding realities to do less and do it well and to set priorities based on key criteria and have more realistic and achievable goals. It is essential that adequate programme guidelines be given to the ninth assembly in order for the Council to have an achievable and appropriate set of programme initiatives for the period following that assembly.

In summary this evaluation points to the need for the WCC to build its programme work around five core functions that need to be addressed globally. Throughout the report we have stated the need for good foundational study and theological grounding for the work undertaken; the importance of advocacy work that enables the prophetic voice of the churches to be heard; the expressed need of the constituency for capacity-building; and repeatedly the need for the Council to build and nurture relationships with and between the churches and the wider constituency. The Council must wisely and carefully steward the human, financial and physical resources that have been entrusted to it. All this needs to be communicated in a timely and imaginative way.

In summary, a culture of transformation needs to be embraced by the staff and the constituency. Such a renewal has to address fundamental issues in the culture of the organization in its ways of thinking, acting and relating.

Notes:
1. Our team has understood the term constituency in a wide sense in the spirit of the CUV. While the major emphasis was on member churches, the information gathering also encompassed NCCs, members of commissions and advisory groups some of whom were not from member churches, CWCs, REOs.
2. The staff leadership group is composed of the general secretary, deputy general secretary, director of programmes, director of

management and the executive secretary in the General Secretariat.
3. Quotations in italics throughout this summary are from constituency responses.
4. CUV is a policy statement adopted by the central committee in 1997.
5. Governing bodies: the central committee on the advice of its programme committee has responsibility to initiate and terminate programmes. The executive committee is responsible for monitoring programmes and activities.

Recommendations Adopted by the Central Committee, February 2005

Note: The evaluation team has chosen not to repeat their recommendations as these were presented and discussed at the programme committee in sufficient detail. We have therefore provided an extract of the recommendations as adopted by the central committee.

Pre-assembly programme evaluation

1 Purpose and vision

The **primary purpose** of the WCC is expressed in the constitution as:
Para III: Purposes and functions
"The primary purpose of the fellowship of churches in the World Council of Churches is to call one another to visible unity in one faith and in one eucharistic fellowship, expressed in worship and common life in Christ, through witness and service to the world, and to advance towards that unity in order that the world may believe."

The programme committee believes that the CUV (Common Understanding and Vision document), adopted by the Harare assembly in 1998, amplifies the constitutional vision for the WCC as a fellowship of churches. Recognizing that the pre-assembly evaluation report highlights that this document is not well known in the member-church constituency, the **Programme Committee recommends** that:

- the central committee reaffirm the CUV document as an expression of the vision of the WCC as a fellowship of churches;
- ways be found to make the document more easily accessible so as to facilitate greater ownership of this vision.

The programme committee draws attention again to paragraph III of the constitution. Beyond stating the primary purpose, it says:

In seeking koinonia in faith and life, witness and service, the churches through the Council will:
- promote the prayerful search for forgiveness and reconciliation in a spirit of mutual accountability, the development of deeper relationships through theological dialogue and the sharing of human, spiritual and material resources with one another;
- facilitate common witness in each place and in all places, and support each other in their work for mission and evangelism;
- express their commitment to diakonia in serving human need, breaking down barriers between people, promoting one human family in justice and peace, and upholding the integrity of creation, so that all may experience the fullness of life;
- nurture the growth of an ecumenical consciousness through pro-

213

cesses of education and a vision of life in community rooted in each particular cultural context;

- assist each other in their relationships to and with people of other faith communities;
- foster renewal and growth in unity, worship, mission and service.

These purposes and functions demonstrate the breadth of the vision of the WCC and provide a foundation for the programmatic work of the Council.

2 Unique role of the WCC

At the same time that this breadth of vision exists, the pre-assembly programme evaluation has clearly heard the call for the WCC to do less, yet with sharper focus, and to do it well. A key question is what can the WCC do, uniquely, as a global fellowship of churches?

The **Programme Committee recommends** that a fourfold strategic focus be adopted as the means by which the Council can develop greater clarity and coherence in its unique role as a global fellowship of churches.

Fourfold strategic focus:
- First, deepening the fellowship through developing clear theological foundations, enabling study and reflection from a variety of perspectives to be brought into dialogue and relationship together.
- Second, enhance the role of the churches in speaking out together and enabling others to speak out in ways that may become seen as

prophetic, or in advocacy with those whose voices are not always easily heard.
- Third, by listening to, reflecting with, accompanying and challenging:
  - the member and associate member church constituency – nurturing relationships;
  - the wider constituency – as represented by the mapping exercise of the reconfiguration process;
  - the wider world – as an international body with links to global organizations and, at the other end of the spectrum, with grassroots movements, both secular and related to other faith communities.
- Fourth, by facilitating a stewardship of ecumenical resources – seeing collaboratively the human, financial and physical resources as an integral part of any accountable programme work.

Whilst any particular **programme or activity** of the WCC may most clearly relate to one of the above, the programme committee believes that it is important that **every programme** relate in some way to all four of these. Additionally, the fourfold strategic focus provides an internal coherence for the total programming through any one of these four approaches. It provides a mind-set within which the detailed planning, monitoring and evaluating of programme work is to be carried out.

3 Assembly responsibilities

The programme committee gave consideration to the mandate for the assembly programme guidelines

214

committee (APGC). It noted that it is the task of the **assembly** "to determine the overall policies of the World Council and to review programmes undertaken to implement policies previously adopted" [Constitution V. 1.c.4] .

The APGC is mandated to propose policies for all further programme work of the WCC. In doing so, the APGC may give examples of programmes which would follow the policy. However, it is not the task of the APGC to propose programmes.

The programme committee recommends that the APGC:

1) review the programmatic work of the WCC using the report *From Harare to Porto Alegre*;

2) receive the pre-assembly evaluation report, parts 1 and 2, and an amended part 3;

3) propose overall policies for future programme work;

4) look broadly at possible priorities for future work in light of the assembly mandate;

5) propose ways of working with its report in the period prior to the September 2006 central committee meeting.

For the sake of continuity of the programmatic life of the Council and an understanding of respective roles, and of the fourfold strategic focus, the programme committee also recommends that at least three members of the current programme committee be nominated by the executive committee to serve on the APGC.

4 Anticipating programmatic design and staffing in 2006 and in the post-assembly period

The period between the assembly and the 2006 central committee meeting will be a necessary time for the staff to focus upon developing and providing programmatic design proposals for the 2006 central committee.

The **programme committee recommends** that:

the work of the staff during that period from the assembly until the September central committee meeting be in the light of the following:

• policies established by the assembly;

• a review and carrying out of the process to close programmes from the period before Porto Alegre that should not be continued as a result of assembly actions and new directions;

• attention to effective methodologies in light of the fourfold strategic focus, including giving special attention to the networks methodology utilized in the DOV process;

• plans clearly in line with the financial resource forecasts provided by the WCC income coordination and development office and the finance committee;

• the building of a clear, well-functioning planning, monitoring and evaluation mechanism that is principally a tool for joint learning, self-analysis, reflection and improvement;

• consideration of the possible need and the wisdom of conducting external evaluation of programming not recently evaluated and that is continuing.

The **programme committee also recommends** that:

the staff leadership group act upon the WCC pre-assembly evaluation management report and report to the executive committee concerning its implementation.

5 Additional recommendations

The programme committee recommends that:

The staff leadership group prepare documented proposals for consideration by the programme committee to:

- clearly define issues that are (a) of a long term nature, (b) time-bound, and (c) specific/urgent;
- make documented choices about priorities based on:
  - core competence
  - listening to and involving the constituency
  - what is best done globally
  - funding realities;
- build in a clear exit strategy – plan the phasing out/reconfiguring/reshaping in all programme designs;
- ensure that there is a communication strategy developed relative to each programme and carried out in the various constituencies.

IMPRIMERIE
LUSSAUD
OFFSET&NUMERIQUE

L'impression et le façonnage
de cet ouvrage
ont été effectués
à l'Imprimerie LUSSAUD
85200 Fontenay-le-Comte

Dépôt légal 4e trimestre 2005
n° 3981
N° d'impression : 204 230